LIVING WITH TERRORISM

by the same author

ACROSS THE RIVER (as Richard Jocelyn)
THE LONG LONG WAR
PROTEST AND THE URBAN GUERRILLA
RIOT AND REVOLUTION IN SINGAPORE AND MALAYA

LIVING WITH TERRORISM

Richard Clutterbuck

RLINGTON HOUSE
PUBLISHERS
NEW ROCHELLE, NEW YORK

To
SIR GEOFFREY JACKSON
who showed the world how to
live with terrorism

Contents

III. BOMBS

IV. HIJACKING

Preface

TERRORISM is a matter of flesh and blood. This was brought home vividly to every British household by press and television pictures of the torn bodies of the victims of two time-bombs placed in crowded Birmingham pubs on 21 November 1974, killing 20 people and wounding another 180.

Everyone today lives under the threat of terrorist violence—children bombed while visiting the Tower of London as much as hijacked air travellers or business executives kidnapped for ransom in Latin America. No one can be wholly protected from terrorism in a free society, and this book can aim no higher than to help people to live with it, rather than die from it. It also searches for some signposts—and there are some quite promising ones—to enable the world to find a way of ridding itself of the disease—as it rid itself of maritime piracy two centuries ago.

The first essential for living with terrorism is to understand it; to understand how terrorists work, and why; to understand the anatomy of their operations and their weapons and techniques; to understand their difficulties and their weak points; and to understand the technical and tactical methods available for defence against them. The citizen in a society under attack needs to know how to make himself less of a target and how to help the police and security forces to protect him.

This book is intentionally brief. The people most under threat are the busiest people. For those who want to study any or all of the various kinds of terrorism in more depth there are some excellent books available.

About kidnapping there is no book to compare with Sir Geoffrey Jackson's *People's Prison* (London, Faber and Faber, 1973).[1] Sir Geoffrey, as British ambassador to Uruguay, was kidnapped in 1971 and held for eight months by a student marxist

1. Also published in the U.S.A. as *Surviving the long Night* (New York, Vanguard Press, 1974).

15

group—the Tupamaros. In his book he gives a detailed description of his kidnapping, and some invaluable advice on how to spot that a kidnapping is being planned. He tells us how he survived his imprisonment, both mentally and physically, and he also throws a revealing light on the psychology and motivation of the terrorist. Like many others I have been inspired by his book, on which I have drawn heavily in writing mine. I am deeply grateful for this inspiration and for the time that Sir Geoffrey has given up to talking to me. If I have got anything wrong, the fault is mine and not his.

About bombs there is less written. There is a natural reluctance to disseminate the techniques for making bombs, though there are several books designed for just this purpose available from revolutionary sources. I have confined my own treatment of this subject to describing enough of how the various kinds of bombs and fuses work in order to help a potential victim to detect them and to know what to avoid if he comes across one. It is very rare for anyone to be killed by a bomb once he has detected that it is there.

Books about security and its hardware are also understandably restricted. The best sources of detailed information are the security firms and security consultants, whose addresses can be found in the Yellow Pages. Before releasing such information these firms will, quite properly, require to know something about the applicant and the uses to which he will put it.

There are two excellent books on hijacking. David Phillips, in *Skyjack* (London, Harrap, 1973) presents a fascinating history of the subject and a series of detailed case studies of a large number of hijackings. Peter Clyne, in *An Anatomy of Skyjacking* (London, Abelard-Schuman, 1973) gives a full account of two famous air piracy trials which are very revealing, and he also offers a constructive plan for dealing with hijacking.

In this book I have tried to gather the essentials of all these subjects together—kidnapping, assassination, bombing and hijacking—in a convenient form. It is the first book-length product of a two and a half year grant made to me in July 1973 by the Social Science Research Council to study political violence. The main function of the grant is to provide me with a research assistant, Miss Nicola Ratcliffe, who has now worked with me for a year and who has contributed a great deal to this book. I am most grateful to her and to the SSRC.

One of the reasons why terrorism is such a virulent poison is that the cure can damage society as much as the disease can. As well as considering how to live with terrorism, I have described some of the measures to which a society may be driven to defend itself against it. In some countries an exaggeration, amounting almost to a fantasy, of terrorism has been built up as an excuse to justify oppressive measures by governments determined to keep their populations firmly controlled in order to preserve the *status quo*. In the name of preventing a dictatorship of the left, there emerges a dictatorship of the right and the two can be almost indistinguishable.

Most commonly, however, terrorism generates its own backlash; when an exasperated public takes the law into its own hands or clamours for tougher action by its government, accepting curtailment of its own liberties. It is this backlash, and very seldom any kind of liberal or progressive change, which is the usual result of terrorist violence.

Many emergency powers, including the suspension of trial by jury for terrorist offences, have had to be introduced in Northern Ireland. The violence there has been no fantasy, but a vicious campaign of killing and intimidation by terrorists of both Catholic and Protestant religion and of both left-wing and right-wing extremes. In Great Britain itself, despite the public fury aroused by the November bombs in Birmingham only the mildest of emergency measures were introduced. One of the reasons for urgency in checking terrorism is to ensure that the quality of our own lives, and our personal freedoms, are not eroded by the kind of measures introduced in some Latin American countries, for this is just the effect that the groups which support terrorism in Britain would like to see.

Exeter, December 1974   RICHARD CLUTTERBUCK

I. INTRODUCTION

Chapter One

The Cult of The Urban Guerrilla

THE URBAN GUERRILLA AND HIS PHILOSOPHY

SINCE 1968 there have been more than 300 attempted hijackings of which about 170 have been successful. There have been over 50 major political kidnappings and hundreds of other kidnappings which, though classed primarily as criminal (i.e. for personal gain), had some political overtones. Political assassinations have been too numerous to record and it is even more difficult to differentiate between political, criminal and other motives in the case of killings.

The present cult of the urban guerrilla dates from the death of Che Guevara. Guevara was a heroic character. He gave up the secure position he had earned in Cuba to die for his ideals in a remote part of Bolivia in October 1967. Rejecting Mao's belief in the need for a mass organization in the villages, he contended that the guerrillas had merely to establish an aggressive *foco* for the people to rise spontaneously in their support.[1] This had appeared to work in Cuba in 1957–58, but in fact the deduction was a false one, because the Batista Government had been so rotten and the morale of its soldiers and provincial officials so low, that Castro's and Guevara's guerrillas were able more or less to walk into a void in the rural areas without any need for mass organization. They then tried to export the *foco* theory to other Latin American countries, but rural guerrillas suffered a series of defeats—in Colombia, Guatemala, Peru and Venezuela; also, agonizingly, under Guevara's personal leadership in Bolivia, where he was unable to attract any popular support at all.

1. Régis Debray, *Revolution in the Revolution?* (London, Penguin, 1967).

21

Guevara by this time had become a hero and it was hard for his disciples to accept that he was wrong; therefore it must be the masses amongst whom he worked who were wrong—the Bolivian peasants. The guerrillas had therefore to take their *foco* into more fertile ground—to the intellectuals and the proletariat. The urban guerrillas are simply the *focos* transferred to the city. They have generally adhered to Debray's philosophy of devoting little attention to organizing popular support, hoping for a spontaneous response to the publicity they can attract by bold and spectacular operations, and relying on funds not on contributions from the masse; but on bank robberies and ransoms.

As well as extorting money and exerting political blackmail (e.g. for the release of prisoners or for changes in the law), the urban guerrilla aims specifically to provoke repression by making it impossible for the government to govern without it, so that the people are harassed by searches, curfews, arrests and detentions; by disruption and unemployment and by a feeling of fear and insecurity. One of their leading philosophers, Carlos Marighela,[2] frankly described the purpose as to make life 'unbearable' for the ordinary people, in the hope that they would become embittered and exasperated with their government and clamour for change. This could conceivably lead to the seizure of power by the guerrillas themselves in what has been well described as a 'climate of collapse'.[3] More commonly there emerges either a weak popular front government which is ready to dance to the guerrillas' tune or—most often of all—there is a military *coup* after which the repression becomes greater still and the whole process starts a new cycle.

The cult of the urban guerrilla has now spread far and wide from Latin America. The Palestinians, smarting from the lack of success of their rural raids on Israeli territory, and deprived of their frontier bases after the 1967 war, began in 1968 to emulate the Latin American urban guerrillas by attacks in the cities of the Western world and in aircraft emanating from these cities. Hijacking by a variety of people with different motives rose sharply in 1968 and 1969. Groups of European university students,

2. Carlos Marighela, *For the Liberation of Brazil* (London, Penguin, 1971).
3. Robert Taber, *The War of the Flea* (London, Paladin, 1970).

branching out impatiently from protest and confrontation on the streets, began to bomb, to shoot and to kidnap. This new manifestation of personal and clandestine violence spread quickly across Europe and America, to London, Los Angeles, Berlin and Istanbul. The terrorist groups began to collaborate increasingly with each other and to seek support from foreign governments where possible, notably from Libya.

Latin America, however, still remained the most active theatre for the urban guerrilla, largely because of the rapid expansion of the cities and of the education system to cope with it. Many young people emerged from universities with an awareness of the inequities in their societies, but saw no avenues open to them in the existing systems for rectifying them. In nations with a long tradition of violence and *machismo*, some of them joined urban guerrilla groups whose aims extended to exerting pressure for internal political change by including concerted campaigns to drive out U.S. business firms, by intimidating or killing their executives and by extorting huge sums from them in ransoms and protection money.

Governments varied in their response to terrorism: Israel was uncompromising; Turkey and Canada stood firm; Brazil and Uruguay moved from appeasement to counter-attack; West Germany was weak and became a regular victim; the U.S. Government was tough in resisting blackmail over its kidnapped diplomats, but American business firms seemed ready to pay up. By early 1974 one Latin American guerrilla group had accumulated a total of $30 million in ransoms. Such tremendous pickings increasingly attracted the criminal world, and the cult of the urban guerrilla became big business.

KIDNAPPING, ASSASSINATION, BLACKMAIL AND RANSOM

Kidnapping for ransom is nothing new. It has been endemic in America for generations and in East Asia for centuries. The kidnapping and murder of the Lindbergh baby in 1932 drove the U.S. Government into making kidnapping a capital offence. Assassinations, also, are as old as civilization. There have, however, been some significant changes since the advent of the urban guerrilla in 1967. Before that, *political* kidnappings were rare. Almost all kidnappings were then for criminal gain—as indeed the great majority still are. In the 50 major *political* kidnappings since 1968, however, the primary aim has usually been to exert coercion or blackmail on governments or commercial firms, with ransom or protection money as a secondary aim.

Recent political murders can be subdivided into mass and often indiscriminate killings, most of which have been by the Palestinians or the IRA, and assassinations of selected individuals, chosen by virtue of their office, for specific political ends. Only the latter can properly be classed as political assassinations. With a small number of exceptions (such as the killing of the Jordanian prime minister in Cairo), most have been directly connected with kidnapping and have usually begun as kidnap attempts. Some have occurred when the government or firm concerned refused to submit to the blackmail; others when the police found and attacked the place where the victim was held; and others in the confusion of the kidnap attempt itself.

Another new dimension, which has applied to many of the mass killings as well as to the political assassinations and kidnappings, has arisen from the enormous power of television. Within hours, any spectacular kidnapping or attack has become known to millions of people. Where there is political blackmail, the kidnappers' demands themselves receive wide publicity. Negotiations for the life of the victim are conducted in an atmosphere of ghoulish public curiosity, apprehension or even hysteria. There is an underlying implication that to refuse to pay is tantamount to pricing the victim's life below the figure demanded. Because of the publicity, the negotiating authorities have to accept that such a refusal may have a vastly magnified effect on the confidence of other potential victims—diplomats, business executives etc. Thus, whereas a government at war will contemptuously reject an ultimatum in the knowledge that the rejection may cost 10,000 lives in the bombardment of a city under siege, the same government may pay a huge political price to save a single life in the face of an ultimatum from a group of three or four clandestine terrorists.

The urban guerrilla is well aware of the power which this gives him. Sometimes a whole operation is mounted solely for the publicity. This now has a name in revolutionary terminology— 'armed propaganda'. The best example of it was at the Munich Olympic Games in September 1972, when eight Arab terrorists kidnapped and killed eleven Israeli athletes. The terrorists can have had no serious expectations of the Israeli government giving way, but some 500 million people, all over the world, watched the drama on television, relayed from Munich to their homes by satellite. Ninety-nine per cent of these viewers were probably disgusted, but a large proportion of them may have had no knowledge at all of the Palestinian cause before this, and it was this that the guerrillas specifically aimed to change. And if they struck a spark of sympathy amongst a tiny percentage—perhaps amongst young people previously unawakened and now drawn by the prospect of a violent and adventurous attack on a world society which they found unsatisfactory—even this tiny per- centage of 500 million could amount to a large number of poten- tial collaborators all over the world.

BOMBS

There is much less risk—though also much less prospect of publicity—in attacking a victim by posting him an explosive letter or parcel than in trying to kidnap him. The coercion of governments and the provocation of repression may be achieved more safely by planting a time bomb than by an orgy of shooting. Though again, it is the mass killings by men with guns rather than by bombs which makes for drama and therefore for publicity.

The 'letter bomb' is one of the meanest and most cowardly of all forms of attack. The person most at risk is probably an inno- cent sorter in the post office; next in line is usually an office clerk or secretary—for the targets tend to be men in public or executive positions. 'Letter bombs' can be lethal, as in the case of an Israeli embassy official in London in 1973. More often they maim, and contribute nothing more than a minor nuisance towards the disruption of confidence which Marighela's disciples are seeking.

The 'shopping bag bomb' in pubs, bus stations etc., and the 'suitcase bomb' in public transport, aircraft or baggage rooms, again aim at disruption and public anxiety. More specifically they aim at making it impossible for the government to avoid the public harassment—through checks, searches, restrictions on checking in baggage, and curfews—which it is hoped will contribute to friction between the public and the government's security forces.

Its bigger brother—the 'car bomb'—is more commonly aimed at disrupting industry, thereby causing immediate unemployment in the short term and increasing it still further in the long term by deterring investment. All of this, it is hoped, will lead to the 'climate of collapse' which Marighela saw as the prelude to cataclysmic change. Whether this change takes the form of surrender or reaction, Marighela claimed that either would suit him well, for the one leads to more scope for disruption, and the other to the eventual creation of still more bitterness caused by greater repression and harassment.

The bomber, if he is caught, is probably more hated than the gunman, as his commonest victims tend to be innocent women and children. His bombing is therefore the form of terrorism most likely to bring a clamour for the death penalty. This especially pleases the guerrilla leaders who launch the bombers on their missions, knowing that executions create martyrs and martyrs are the best recruiters for support amongst that small element of the population who are potential sympathizers—the people to whom the urban guerrilla has a romantic and heroic appeal.

HIJACKING

The hijacker hits modern society at its most vulnerable. Almost every government and airline has to accept that once a hijack team gains armed control of a modern airliner, they will have to submit to the hijackers' demands at least in so far as it is necessary to get the aircraft and its passengers safely on to the ground. Thereafter, governments have varied widely in their treatment. At Lod Airport on 9th May 1972 the Israelis launched a successful frontal attack on a hijacked aircraft on the ground by using commandos disguised as mechanics. Some Arab governments, becoming exasperated with Palestinian hijackers, have isolated and besieged the grounded aircraft until the hijackers have submitted to arrest. Other governments—the majority—have succumbed, given the hijackers what they demanded, and allowed them to fly away.

Apart from human lives, huge sums of money are at stake. When the Palestinian terrorists blew up three aircraft at Dawson's Field, in Jordan, in September 1972, the cost to the insurance underwriters was $35 million. A Jumbo jet costs about $20 million.

Great progress, however, has been made since 1972 in the countering of hijacking—which was in fact put in motion in response to the Dawson's Field incident. The number of successful hijackings has been drastically cut down and this in turn has led to a big fall in the number of attempts. There is nothing which fails like failure. The success in countering hijacking has resulted from a realization of the right point at which to attack it, and this will be described in a later chapter. Equally significant has been the growing disenchantment of some of the governments which have in the past encouraged or connived at hijackings, notably the Cuban and some of the Arab governments. These successes offer a heartening gleam of encouragement in the battle to counter other forms of terrorism too.

TERRORISTS—WHO, WHY AND HOW?

Terrorists, without exception, claim to speak and fight on behalf of the working classes—the proletariat and the peasants. Yet with very rare exceptions (such as the Provisional IRA) they are led and predominantly recruited from university students, graduates and the sons and daughters of the affluent. They make the most of the few working-class recruits whom they do manage to attract into their ranks, and especially so where these come from the deprived or coloured communities—as, for example, in the Symbionese Liberation Army (SLA) in California which kidnapped Patricia Hearst in 1974. Sadly, most of these few recruits from poor backgrounds are enlisted from among the criminal fringes of society or are inadequate, rejected or rootless people who can find nothing else on to which to pin their lives. Terrorist recruits from the farms or the shop floor are almost unknown.

It is a common error to categorize contemptuously the intellectual terrorists themselves as inadequate, nihilistic or pathological. Even though this may in some cases be true, it can be dangerously wrong. Though their total numbers are very small indeed, most of them do, in fact, start out deeply indoctrinated with ideological beliefs and are convinced that what they are doing is in the interest of working people, however much those people may reject them. They really believe that they know better than the 'men on the shop floor'. They are unconscious of the arrogance of this assumption, for they have learned it from the writings of the revolutionaries on whom they model themselves—and especially from Marx and Lenin. It is a mistake to underestimate their conviction of righteousness or to assume that they can be easily deterred from what they believe to be their duty to mankind by the threat of death, imprisonment or economic deprivation. Some of them convince themselves that they should welcome martyrdom as the most effective contribution they can make to their cause. We will look again at their motivation and methods in chapters 10 and 12, but for the moment it suffices to say that the best protection against them comes, not so much from trying to deter them, as from physically denying them access to their targets or to the tools which they need to kill and destroy. They can no more be deterred by reasoning than can a poisonous snake, yet they are harder to keep out than snakes because they have the human intelligence and the means to co-operate with each other, both locally and internationally.

An International, a Corporate and a Personal Problem

Since terrorists collaborate internationally, it is not enough merely to counter them locally; it is necessary to mobilize international collaboration against them. This is easier said than done, because almost every group can find at least one foreign government, as well as fraternal revolutionary groups in other countries, which will sympathize with their aims.

International companies are increasingly becoming prime targets for terrorism, both for ideological reasons and because they offer the best promise of big money. One of the terrorists' main aims is to make it both dangerous and unprofitable for these large companies to operate in the developing world—and especially in Latin America—in order to check the economic growth of both the rich and the poor countries, in the hope that recession in the rich countries will cause the bitterness and disappointed expectations on which revolution thrives; and also in the hope that frustration of development in the poor countries will prevent the formation of the strongest bulwark against revolution—a middle class and a prosperous sector in the working class to which the rest can aspire to join. Put in revolutionary terms, this means the frustration of *bourgeois* aspirations in the rich world in order to breed more revolutionaries amongst both intellectuals and workers; and the removal of a feasible target for *bourgeois* aspirations in the developing world in order to engender an atmosphere of hopelessness, which should have the same effect.

The overwhelming majority of people, in both rich and poor countries, long for stable government and for greater prosperity. Revolutionaries accept that this is so, but dismiss these aspirations as the product of 'social conditioning' of the mass of the people from birth, by their parents, their schools, their employers, by their governments and their societies, through the media. In fact, this development of a desire for stability and for the expectation of prosperity, this 'social conditioning', can better be described as the process of civilization itself. A process, which has arisen from man's desire and ability to co-operate and to accept some degree of restraint and organization in the realization that this benefits him, his family and the community. It is what differentiates him from the two extremes of the animal kingdom —the anarchy of the jungle on the one hand and on the other, the suppression of the individual in the over-regimentation of the ant-hill. Basically, the anarchist seeks the jungle and the marxist seeks the ant-hill. To avoid these extremes, communities must protect themselves, must collaborate internationally, and must continue the international growth and the spread of wealth which gives the individual the prospect of better things, and which in turn has provided both the motivation and the bulwark of civilization.

The front line in this battle is held, even more so than in other kinds of war, by individuals in isolation or in small groups. Sometimes—like the victims of hijacking or car-bombs—they have to protect themselves collectively. More commonly the decisive front-line battles are fought by men and women facing their enemy alone—the men and women who are the targets for personal attack, by kidnapping, by assassination or by letters or parcels through the mail. These front-line fighters are the exponents of the civilization which the terrorists aim to destroy—statesmen, diplomats, officials and executives. In more conventional wars a thousand deaths or a thousand captures may have little significance. The circumstances of the new war resemble ancient times when battles could be decided by single combat. The spectacular killing or capture of one individual can strike terror into the hearts of a million others. A capitulation to blackmail or ransom can inspire other terrorist groups, and can erode the confidence of civilized communities throughout the world. This book is, for the most part, concerned with how best the individual can fight his often lonely battle, and how the rest of the community can best support him in his fight.

II. KIDNAPPING, ASSASSINATION, BLACKMAIL AND RANSOM

suffered a severe defeat in 1967 and this was attributed largely to counter-insurgency techniques taught by U.S. military assistance and advisory groups (MAAGs) which had been formed originally by President Kennedy in 1961-63. Further resentment was aroused by the suspicion that U.S. advisers were responsible for teaching some of the brutal and oppressive measures which the police and the army were using to fight the guerrillas.

On 16th January 1968 two U.S. officers of the MAAG in Guatemala, Colonel John D. Webber and Lieutenant-commander Ernest A. Munro, were shot dead from a passing car while returning from lunch in what appeared to be an attempted kidnap. The Fuerzas Armadas Rebeldes (FAR) claimed responsibility.

Seven months later (on 28th August 1968) the U.S. ambassador to Guatemala, John G. Mein, was killed in a kidnap attempt when his official car was blocked in and surrounded by uniformed guerrillas while he was returning to his office from an official luncheon in the Embassy Residence. The FAR claimed that he had been killed 'while resisting political kidnapping'—their intention being to hold him as hostage for the release of their own commandant, Camilo Sanchez, who had recently been captured.

The Government during this period was a relatively liberal one under President Julio César Méndez Montenegro, who found himself unable to control the growth of a number of right-wing terrorist groups which began to take the law into their own hands, themselves kidnapping the archbishop of Guatemala City whom they accused of connivance with the left-wing guerrillas.

Meanwhile there had been a number of spectacular kidnappings by left-wing guerrillas in Brazil, in which the Government had given way and these may have influenced President Méndez— coupled with his fear of further right-wing backlash—in standing firm when the West German ambassador, Count von Spreti, was kidnapped on 31st March 1970[1] from his official car in downtown Guatemala City between the Embassy and his home. The FAR demanded the release of 17 prisoners and a ransom of $700,000.

The Government refused to do this on the grounds that some of the prisoners had been convicted and that the executive had no power to overrule the judiciary. They launched an all-out attack

1. Robert Moss, *Urban Guerrillas* (London, Temple Smith, 1972).

on the FAR, accompanied by drastic measures for population control. The West German Government applied pressure on the Guatemalan Government to release the prisoners, but they stood firm and von Spreti was killed on the expiry of the terrorists' ultimatum on 4th April. The German Government virtually cut off diplomatic relations and asked the Guatemalan ambassador to leave.

Shortly afterwards Méndez was replaced as president by Colonel Arana Osorio, who had conducted the successful campaign against the rural guerrillas in 1967. Arana maintained his offensive against the FAR, whose activities appear to have been completely suppressed. Some of the right-wing terrorist groups have continued to operate, however, and it has been suggested that these have been condoned and even institutionalized by the Guatemalan Government.[2] Civil liberties remain drastically restricted, and the FAR campaign appears to have had one of the commonest effects of revolutionary terror—a right-wing backlash and a disagreeable erosion of the quality of life. Whether this 'oppression' will have the effect predicted by Carlos Marighela remains to be seen.

BRAZIL

On 4th September 1969 the U.S. ambassador to Brazil, Charles Burke Elbrick, was kidnapped when four gunmen held up his car in Rio de Janeiro while he was returning to his office from lunch in his Residence. The kidnappers demanded the release of 15 prisoners and the broadcast of a manifesto. The Government submitted to both demands and Elbrick was released.

Six months later (on 11th March 1970) the Japanese consul general in São Paulo was kidnapped on his way home from his office. The Government again gave way, and the consul general was released in exchange for five prisoners.

On 5th April 1970 the U.S. consul general in Porto Allegro was wounded while successfully resisting an attempt to kidnap him from his car; but on 16th June the Brazilian Government

2. Kenneth Johnson, *Guatemala: From Terrorism to Terror* (London Institute for the Study of Conflict, 1972).

released 40 prisoners in exchange for the West German ambassador. This incident occurred a few weeks after the kidnap and murder of the German ambassador to Guatemala, Count von Spreti. Finally, in January 1971, the Brazilian Government released 70 prisoners in exchange for the Swiss ambassador, kidnapped 40 days earlier.

It was widely predicted that this escalation of ransoms would continue, but these predictions proved wrong. The Brazilians, like the Guatemalans, cracked down hard on the terrorists and took tough measures to deny them public support. As in Guatemala there were unpleasant stories of torture, and counter-terrorism. Terrorists, in both countries, tend to 'mysteriously disappear' and civil liberties cannot be compared with those surviving in Britain and the United States. On the other hand, Brazil has one of the highest economic growth rates in the world; inflation has been controlled even if not cured. Outwardly Brazil appears to be one of the most prosperous and stable of Latin American countries. As in Guatemala, only time will tell whether the price paid in the erosion of the quality of life proves too high for the stability to last.

URUGUAY

Like their comrades in Guatemala and Brazil, the Tupamaros in Uruguay provoked a backlash which led to their virtual destruction in 1972, but during 1968–71 they had earned themselves the reputation of being the most successful of all urban guerrilla movements. From the start they cultivated a 'Robin Hood' image, since copied by many others. They also demonstrated that kidnapping Uruguayan citizens could humiliate the Government more than kidnapping foreigners.

Their first political kidnapping was of Ulises Pereyra Reverbel, a close friend of the president, in August 1968. They later released him and kidnapped him a second time as a display of their dominance over the Government. They also kidnapped a banker in 1969 to show solidarity with striking bank employees and again released him when it suited them.[3] It was not until 1970 that they

3. Moss, *op. cit.*

began to kidnap diplomats, following the fashion established in Guatemala and Brazil, beginning the simultaneous kidnapping on 31st July of the Brazilian consul, Dias Gomides, and of two American officials, Gordon Jones and Dan Mitrione.

The Brazilian consul was kidnapped by Tupamaros who entered his home disguised as repair men. He was released on 21st February 1971 after payment of a ransom of $250,000.[4]

Gordon Jones, a young U.S. diplomat, was kidnapped on the same day by Tupamaros who ambushed him in his garage when he was about to drive to work. He was trussed in sacking 'like a side of bacon' but managed to escape by a remarkable gymnastic feat—flipping over the tail-board of a truck in a busy street.[5]

Dan Mitrione, an American police adviser, was kidnapped— also on 31st July 1970—while being driven to work in his official car. A fourth man, Dr. Claude Fly, an American agricultural adviser, was kidnapped by five men who burst into his laboratory office on 7th August, possibly looking for someone to replace Gordon Jones. He was released on 21st March when a doctor (kidnapped specially by the Tupamaros) reported that he was likely to die of heart failure if his imprisonment continued.

For Mitrione and Fly the Tupamaros demanded the release of 150 of their members from prison. When this request was refused Mitrione was shot dead and his body found in a car on 10th August—three days after the kidnapping of Dr. Fly. Mitrione was the father of nine children and, despite the assumption that he was a member of the CIA, his murder caused a powerfully adverse reaction amongst the Uruguayan public[6] which created serious misgivings amongst the Tupamaros themselves.[7]

On 8th January 1971 the British ambassador, Geoffrey Jackson, was kidnapped on his way from his home to the Embassy in Montevideo in his official car. He has given a detailed account of his kidnapping and imprisonment in his book, *People's Prison*,

4. Congressional Committee Staff Study, *Political Kidnappings 1968–73* (Washington D.C., 1973, p. 18).
5. Geoffrey Jackson, *People's Prison* (London, Faber and Faber, 1973, p. 19).
6. *Political Kidnappings* (p. 18).
7. Jackson, *op. cit.* (p. 20).

and this will be examined further in a later chapter. The price of his release was declared to be the release of the same 150 prisoners as were demanded for Mitrione and Fly, but the public reaction to Mitrione's murder made the Tupamaros reluctant to commit another when this demand was ignored. The British ambassador was released on 9th September 1971, three days after a spectacular jail-break in which 106 of the 150 Tupamaro prisoners escaped.[8] A Tupamaro communiqué announced that his retention 'served no further purpose'.

Three months later there was a general election in Uruguay. The left-wing *Frente Amplio*, a coalition similar to Allendé's in Chile, lost much of the support which it had enjoyed in public opinion polls a year earlier. The Tupamaros had supported the *Frente*, but their 'Robin Hood' image had died with Dan Mitrione and their claim of infallibility had been deflated by Geoffrey Jackson. Their support proved to be a kiss of death. The new president was elected with a mandate to deal with them. When they made the further mistake of attacking the army, the army in turn demanded, and was given, full control over internal security. Within a year all but a handful of Tupamaros had been killed or captured—though the ransom money earned by Argentinian guerrillas is being used in an attempt to revive the movement. As in Guatemala and Brazil, however, the only real achievement of the Tupamaros has been to erode the quality of life — unrelieved, in the case of Uruguay, by any promise of a prosperity like Brazil's.

Canada

Canada offers an example of the government acting firmly and quickly, but with a sensible degree of compromise which resulted in the virtual elimination of a terrorist movement without permanent damage to the way of life.

On 5th October 1970, following the Latin American fashion, five armed men of the Front de Libération du Québec (FLQ) broke into the home of a British diplomat in Montreal, James

8. Moss, *op. cit.* (p. 229).

Cross, and kidnapped him. They demanded the release of 13 prisoners, a ransom of $500,000 in gold and the publication of an FLQ manifesto. They also demanded the name of the informant whose tip-off had led to a police raid on the FLQ three months earlier.

On 10th October the FLQ kidnapped Pierre Laporte, a minister in the Provincial Government of Quebec, while he was crossing the street outside his home. They declared that they would kill him unless the demands made for the release of Cross were met.

Prime Minister Trudeau obtained overwhelming support in the Federal Parliament for the introduction on 16th October of the War Measures Act, declaring the terrorists to be armed belligerents, and placing Canada on a war footing to defeat them. Thousands of soldiers were deployed in the streets and hundreds of people were arrested. Trudeau made a tough speech on television:

> 'There are a lot of bleeding hearts around who just don't like to see people with helmets and guns. All I can say is, go on and bleed, but it is more important to keep law and order in the society than to be worried about weak-kneed people . . . I think society must take every means at its disposal to defend itself against the emergence of a parallel power which defies the elected power in this country.'[9]

Pierre Laporte was strangled with the chain of his crucifix, and his body found in a car on 18th October. In the course of questioning suspects arrested under the War Measures Act, the Government ascertained that the two kidnappings were by different factions of the FLQ. The faction which held Cross had attempted to moderate the demands, but had been overruled by the other. Trudeau showed his flexibility by agreeing to transport three kidnappers and four of their relatives to Cuba in a Canadian Forces plane and Cross was released on 3rd December 1970.[10]

Trudeau's mixture of ruthlessness and compromise gained him massive popular support. In subsequent local elections in Quebec, parties which had shown sympathy for the FLQ lost heavily and

9. Quoted by Moss, *op. cit.* (p. 127).
10. *Political Kidnappings* (p. 20).

the FLQ themselves—at one time a powerful and well-organized movement—have not reappeared. The War Measures Act was lifted in April 1971 and life in Canada resumed its normal pace.

TURKEY

Another government which has stood firm is that of Turkey, though it cannot be suggested that life there is as free as in Canada.

On 4th March 1971 four American airmen driving home from a NATO radar station near Ankara in the early morning were held up by a roadblock and when they got out to remove it they were kidnapped by armed terrorists. The kidnappers demanded a ransom of 400,000 Turkish *lira* and the publication of a manifesto. The police, however, arrested a man trying to park the airmen's car and he revealed the names of four others. All were present or former university students. The airmen were released on 8th March, and 45,000 police and soldiers launched a search for the kidnappers, who were arrested, tried and executed.

On 17th May 1971 four armed terrorists raided the home of the Israeli consul general in Istanbul, Ephraim Elrom, and declared that he would be killed unless all revolutionary guerrillas were released from prison. The Government refused and Elrom was shot, his body being found on 23rd May.

In an intensive search for the kidnappers, Turkish police stormed a building in which two terrorists were holding a 14-year-old girl as a hostage. One was killed and the other was captured, tried for Elrom's murder, and executed.[11]

In March 1972, Turkish guerrillas captured three more NATO technicians—two British and one Canadian. The Turkish police located them and killed or captured all the guerrillas, who had themselves killed the technicians before they were overpowered.

Turkey, like Brazil, Guatemala and Uruguay, has had to pay a price in loss of civil liberties, and there are signs of brittleness in the régime that may spell further trouble ahead. The Turkish Government, however, has shown a ruthlessness in attacking the problem, matched only by the Israelis.

11. *Ibid.* (p. 23).

The Palestinian Guerrillas

The pattern of kidnapping by the Palestinian guerrillas is very different from that of other groups and is frequently combined with hijacking of aircraft. While the Israeli Government has stood firm at whatever cost to Israeli lives, most other governments have not.

The hijacking of three aircraft (American, British and Swiss) to Dawson's Field in Jordan, in September 1970, quickly became a kidnapping when over 400 hostages were held on the ground, initially in the aircraft and later (reduced to 56) in a guerrilla base in a refugee camp. After the three aircraft had been blown up, these 56 hostages were released or rescued, and seven Palestinian prisoners were released. The effect on world opinion was such that King Hussein was able to drive virtually all the guerrillas out of Jordan with scarcely a hand being raised on their behalf, even by other Arab countries.

It was to avenge this, that the Black September Organization (BSO) was formed in 1971. After assassinating the Jordanian prime minister on a visit to Cairo, BSO kidnapped eleven Israeli athletes by raiding their quarters at the Munich Olympic Games on 5th September 1972. Encouraged by the Israeli Government, the Bavarian police attacked them while they were trying to transfer their hostages to an aircraft at Munich airport. All the hostages and five terrorists were killed, the other three being arrested, but later released under threat of destruction of a hijacked German aircraft in the air a few weeks later.

On 1st March 1973, eight BSO terrorists seized the Saudi Arabian Embassy in Khartoum and held two American diplomats, Ambassador Cleo A. Noel and G. Curtis Moore, and the Belgian consul, Guy Eid, as hostages. They demanded the release of 60 Palestinian prisoners held in Jordan and of Sirhan B. Sirhan, the killer of Senator Robert Kennedy in the United States.

President Nixon followed the standard American practice of refusing to yield to blackmail and all three hostages were killed. The terrorists then surrendered to the Sudanese and were charged and tried, but released a year later.

MEXICO

An attempt by the U.S. Government to stand firm was, however, frustrated in Mexico where, on 4th May 1973 the U.S. consul general in Guadalajara, Terence G. Leonhardy, was kidnapped by four armed youths while driving home at night from an official engagement. The terrorists demanded the release of 30 prisoners and the publication of a communiqué. The communiqué was broadcast, but they then added a further demand for a ransom of $80,000. The Mexican Government, which had conceded to previous ransom demands for its own nationals, ordered the 30 prisoners to be released. The U.S. Government objected, reiterating its policy of not yielding to extortion or blackmail for the release of U.S. officials anywhere in the world. Meanwhile Mrs. Leonhardy negotiated a loan from a Mexican state bank to pay the ransom and her husband was released on 6th May.

THE UNITED STATES AND THE UNITED KINGDOM

Though the United States has a high score of criminal kidnappings there have been virtually no political kidnappings. The Symbionese Liberation Army (SLA) tried to put a political gloss on the kidnapping of Patricia Hearst, by making an initial demand for food for the poor, but it soon emerged that it was a straightforward criminal gang at work, with nothing more political in mind than a hatred of the rich. Its interest lay in the apparent conversion of Patricia Hearst to their way of life.

Apart from an abortive attempt in May 1974 by a man with a history of mental illness to kidnap Princess Anne from her car near Buckingham Palace, there have been few political kidnappings as yet in the U.K. either. The abduction of members of rival groups or factions by the IRA or by Protestant terrorists in Northern Ireland fall more into the category of gang warfare and neither these, nor the assassinations of public figures, such as Senator Barnhill, have been accompanied by demands for ransom or by political blackmail. This might well have been otherwise, but for the fact that all British Governments have declared, like the U.S. Government, that they will not pay ransoms or release prisoners in the face of kidnapping. They have further warned that any firm or individual paying money to an illegal organization (such as the IRA) will be prosecuted.

Nor, so far, has kidnapping been used in the U.S.A. or the U.K. to coerce or intimidate commercial firms. This has been the prerogative mainly of one particular terrorist group in Argentina.

Chapter Three

The Attack on Commercial Firms in Argentina

THE DEVELOPMENT OF THE ERP

THE *Ejertico Revolucionario de Pueblo* (ERP) or People's Revolutionary Army, was formed in 1970 as the armed wing of the Trotskyist Revolutionary Workers' Party (PRT). It was affiliated to the Trotskyist Fourth International in Paris and, though it dissociated itself from that body in 1973, it remains Trotskyist in its aims and methods. The PRT is organized into three types of cell: *mass* cells which organize support in factories, universities etc., *apparatus* cells which organize functions such as publishing, and *military* cells which are predominantly responsible for fund raising, by 'expropriations' (i.e. bank robberies) and by ransoms from kidnapping. The *military* cells comprise the ERP.

The ERP welcomes collaboration with groups from other movements, but insists that these groups accept the discipline of the ERP and also accept the formation of a party cell in their unit—in other words, they are absorbed by the ERP.[1] Considerable numbers of guerrillas have recently joined them in this way, mainly Tupamaros in flight from Uruguay in 1972 and Miristas escaping after the military *coup* in Chile in 1973. Thus by 1974 the strength of the ERP was believed to have reached 5,000[2]— exceptionally large for an underground terrorist movement. The

1. *Political Kidnappings* (p. 37).
2. Peter Janke, 'Terrorism in Argentina' in the *Journal of the Royal United Services Institute*, September 1974. The Tupamaros had at their peak claimed a strength of 3,000.

44

ERP, the Tupamaros and the Miristas, along with the *Ejertico de Liberacion Nacional* (ELN) in Bolivia, issued a joint statement of aims in February 1974. Later, after the receipt of a $14·2 million ransom for a kidnap victim in May 1974, the four movements announced that they were to operate a joint command, and to reopen a rural front as well as continuing urban activities.

The first known operation by the ERP was on 18th September 1970 when they attacked the police station at Rosario, killing two policemen. Early in 1971 they seized more than $300,000 in a bank raid in Cordoba. Since then, however, they have switched almost entirely to kidnapping executives of commercial firms for ransom and had by May 1974 accumulated an estimated total of $30 million.

The Cultivation of a 'Robin Hood' Image

On 23rd May 1971, three armed men seized Stanley Sylvester outside his home in Rosario. He was an executive of the Swift Meat Packing Company and was also the honorary British consul. The ERP demanded that the company provide $62,500 for food and clothing for the poor and the company complied. Sylvester was released on 30th May.

On 22nd March 1972 the ERP kidnapped Oberdan Sallustro, a Fiat executive, in Buenos Aires, demanding the release of 50 prisoners and the delivery by the Fiat company of $1 million in the form of exercise books, shoes, pencils and other goods to children in 798 schools in poor districts. The Argentine Government refused to release the prisoners but the Fiat company agreed to pay the ransom. They were, however, warned by the Government that they would be prosecuted for 'illicit associations' unless they immediately broke all contact with the kidnappers.[3] On 10th April the police discovered and attacked the hideout where Sallustro was being held. Four terrorists were captured, but not before they had killed Sallustro.

3. *Political Kidnappings* (p. 24).

The Abandonment of the Mask

On 11th March 1973 the military government in Argentina held elections for a president as the first step towards restoration of civilian rule and the return of ex-President Perón from his exile in Madrid. The Peronist candidate, Hector Campora, was returned and agreed to make way for the re-election of Perón himself. Though the ERP initially announced conditional support for Perón they soon abandoned this and in any case they continued to kidnap expatriate business executives for ransom, though they now more or less abandoned the 'Robin Hood' mask and demanded ever-increasing sums to go into their party funds.

On 2nd April 1973 six terrorists kidnapped Anthony DaCruz from his car near the Kodak plant in Buenos Aires, where he was technical operations manager. They demanded a ransom of $1·5 million which Kodak paid, and DaCruz was released on 7th April.

On 22nd May the ERP made an unsuccessful attempt to kidnap an executive of the Ford Motor Company in Buenos Aires, Luis Giovanelli, as he drove away from the factory. The plant guard intervened and Giovanelli was wounded, but escaped capture. The Ford Motor Company were later reputed to have complied with a demand to pay the ERP $1 million as protection money against a repetition of the attack.

Protection money has often been demanded by revolutionaries, as well as by other criminal gangs, from businesses, large and small, and from individual operators such as truck owners or small shopkeepers. French firms, for example, were believed to pay protection money regularly in Vietnam in order to continue to function. Others find it expedient to do the same all over the world, but seldom on the scale paid to ERP.

On 23rd May 1973 the ERP demanded another $1 million which they declared was 'to help finance the revolutionary struggle'. This was for an Argentine executive, Aaron Bellinson, kidnapped near his home in Buenos Aires. He was released on 3rd June after payment of the ransom.

On 6th June Charles Lockwood, a British executive of Acrow

Steel was kidnapped by four terrorists from his car near his home in a suburb of Buenos Aires. A ransom of $2 million was paid and he was released on 30th June.

On 18th June Mr. John R. Thompson, an American executive of Firestone Tire and Rubber Company, was kidnapped shortly after he had driven out of the plant. Ten armed terrorists used five vehicles to block his car. This was done close to the stands in which crowds, estimated at several millions, were beginning to assemble to greet Juan Perón on his return from Spain two days later. This was the first of a number of incidents staged by revolutionary movements which turned the reception into a bloody shambles in which over 100 people were killed. Thompson was eventually released on 6th July after payment of a then record ransom of $3 million.

On 6th December 1973 an Exxon executive, Victor Samuelson, was kidnapped at the oil refinery of Exxon's subsidiary, Esso Argentina, and was held for nearly five months. The ERP demanded a record ransom of $14·2 million, to be paid partly in goods and partly in money. Exxon paid the ransom in full in March 1974, but the ERP held Samuelson for a further 49 days while they 'laundered' the money to ensure that they could not be traced. He was eventually released on 29th April 1974.

THE AIMS AND PROSPECTS OF THE ERP

It is now clear that from 1970–72 the ERP was primarily concerned with building up its strength and its popular support. This was not difficult while the unpopular military government remained in power, and the demand that ransoms should be paid in food and goods for the poor, and particularly for poor children, built up an initial fund of sympathy. When the military government had announced its intention of paving the way for the return of Perón and of civilian government, the pattern changed. While paying lip service to Peronism in accord with popular enthusiasm, the ERP clearly realized that it was going to be more difficult for them to retain their own support. They therefore changed their tactics—perhaps unwisely—in two respects. First, they channelled their ransom and protection money into funds to finance their revolutionary war, rather than into philanthropic measures to attract popularity. Secondly, they aimed to provoke repression by the Peronist Government in accordance with Carlos Marighela's philosophy.

This began with the violence staged between left- and right-wing groups at Perón's return on 20th June 1973. One of the aims of this was to split the left and right wings of the Peronist Party. Perón and Campora had both initially appeared to favour their left wing against the traditional trade-unionist right wing on which Perón's previous administration in the 1950s had been based. The ERP judged it necessary to force Campora and Perón to the right in order to attact left-wing opinion—and especially student opinion—away from Peronism and to themselves. They therefore began, along with their attacks on executives of foreign firms, to increase their attacks on Argentine executives and officials, army posts and government agencies hoping that the Government, faced with no alternatives other than to accept chaos, would be forced to take repressive measures. By the late summer the ERP were condemning Campora and Perón as fascists and dismissing the elections as a fraud.[4] On 24th September 1973—the day after the election in which Perón was returned, but before he had taken up office, the Government finally outlawed the ERP.

In June 1974 the 78-year-old president died, leaving the Government weak and divided and the ERP rich and strong, dedicated to violent revolution throughout Latin America and with control, both executive and financial, over the ELN, the Miristas and the Tupamaros who were struggling to revive their campaigns in Bolivia, Chile and Uruguay.

THE DILEMMA OF THE INTERNATIONAL CORPORATIONS

As part of these activities, not only in Argentina, but also in other Latin American countries where the ERP influence pertains, the campaign against foreign firms must be expected to intensify.

4. Manifesto reprinted in Kenneth Johnson's *Peronism: The Final Gamble* (London, Institute for the Study of Conflict, January 1974).

The kidnapping of executives has proved far more lucrative than the earlier kidnappings of diplomats and less liable to alienate public sympathy from the terrorists. Already many foreign firms —including Ford and Otis—have largely evacuated their expatriate personnel. Others are paying protection money to the ERP. Nearly all, despairing of the government's ability to protect their staffs and premises, are paying large sums to private security agencies to guard them. Others are paying heavy insurance premiums to cover ransom payments for their executives. Lloyds of London have always been prepared to cover political risks—in the form of nationalization, expropriation, damage or other hazards which can hit assets, production or sales. Premiums vary from country to country with Lloyds' assessment of the risk. In the case of ransom insurance, they will not provide cover if the payment of ransoms to illegal agencies is prohibited by law (as in Northern Ireland) and they will not in any event pay unless the case has been referred to the local government or its police. The knowledge that rich insurance exists is undoubtedly of encouragement to kidnappers, but it is probably fair to say that without it some firms and their executives would not be prepared to operate in Latin America at all.

This, of course, is the declared aim of the ERP—that, by harassment and by the infliction of unacceptable financial loss, they will drive the foreign firms out altogether. One of the effects of this would, of course, be severe recession and unemployment in the Latin American countries themselves. The revolutionary philosophy believes that this creates a revolutionary situation. Sober experience in Latin America, however, suggests that it usually leads to a right-wing military dictatorship.

A compromise solution attempted by some firms is to withdraw all expatriate personnel and even to remove all overt connection with the parent international firm. Thus, the Michegan Motor Company of Argentina would become simply, *Lobezno Compania de Coches*, owned and financed in Michegan, but operated wholly by Argentine personnel in Argentina.

This might alleviate the problem, but it would not solve it. The link, however discreet, could not conceivably be secret. Argentine staffs could be kidnapped—as indeed they are now— and the firms might suffer more local calumny if they would only pay ransoms for expatriates and were ready to abandon a local man to his fate.

What may prove in the end to be a more serious problem is the freedom with which right-wing terrorist groups seem to operate in Argentina.[5] The result can only be an even greater erosion of the freedom of the individual.

The solution can lie only in mobilizing public opinion against every kind of terrorist in their own country. This is not easy. The revolutionaries now have huge funds available for propaganda and this is being lavishly and cleverly used—for example, in financing the highly professional and expensively made films which now regularly appear on television and are playing in cinemas, especially in universities, all over the world. In the short term the provocation of repression—especially if it seems to be imposed to defend the right of *gringos* to exploit local workers—does make Latin American governments unpopular, and one of the possible consequences of this is the emergence of weak popular front governments like Allende's in Chile. Occasionally a progressive military régime can emerge, as in Peru, but Mussolini and Batista were both at first regarded as 'progressive'. In the long run, if events are allowed to take their course, the terrorists will be destroyed. But only at the expense of hardship and loss of liberty for the people of their countries which would be a tragedy for them—and which we have seen happen already in so many countries. It can only be a matter of opinion, as to whether such a right-wing dictatorship with continued commercial co-operation from the outside world, is better or worse than the left-wing dictatorship which would result if—directly or through the historic process of an interim liberal or popular front régime—the terrorists themselves were to gain control.

The firing line against both of these eventualities is held, not so much by soldiers and policemen—albeit on street corners rather than in fortified positions—as by the diplomat or the executive at home or at work or, most hazardously of all, in his car on the way between the two.

5. The correspondent of *The Times* in Buenos Aires was kidnapped in December 1974 by a right-wing terrorist group which warned him that he would be killed if he did not immediately leave the country. He did. *The Times*, 17th December 1974.

Chapter Four

The Journey Between Home and Work

THE MOST VULNERABLE TIME

IN an analysis of 35 major political kidnappings between January 1968 and June 1973,[1] the Committee on Internal Security of the U.S. House of Representatives found that more than half (20) had been of officials or executives in their cars on the way between home and work, or while driving to, or returning from, official functions. Of the remainder, 11 were kidnapped from home and only 2 from their place of work. Two fell into none of these categories (e.g. one was an attaché arriving for his 'customary 6.a.m. calisthenics on the polo field' in Santo Domingo).

Several of the 11 kidnapped at home were in fact ambushed when they were emerging from or re-entering their houses, and these cases were therefore very similar to the kidnappings from cars.

One kidnapping from a car has been recorded in some detail[2] by the victim and his account is most revealing, both of the way in which a terrorist group may prepare for such an operation, and the problems of countering it.

A KIDNAPPING FROM A CAR—GEOFFREY JACKSON

Geoffrey Jackson, then the British ambassador to Uruguay, was kidnapped by the Tupamaros on 8th January 1971 and released after eight months in a 'people's prison'.

1. *Political Kidnappings*, *op. cit.*
2. Geoffrey Jackson, *op. cit.*

He began to sense the likelihood of his being kidnapped quite early in 1970. In March of that year there were six major political kidnappings in Latin America—of a Soviet and a U.S. diplomat in Argentina, of a Japanese consul general in Brazil, of a U.S. attaché in the Dominican Republic and of another U.S. attaché and finally of the West German ambassador in Guatemala. The latter was Count von Spreti, who was killed when the ransom demand was refused by the Guatemalan Government. There were further kidnappings in April, May and June.

On the strength of these and of what appeared to be an attempt to kidnap the Swiss ambassador in Uruguay, Geoffrey Jackson flew to London in June to acquaint the British Foreign Office of the situation and to discuss the action to be taken if he were kidnapped. In particular they agreed that there must be no giving way to blackmail or demands for ransom.

Jackson returned to Montevideo—with his wife, who was a party to these discussions—on the day on which the Tupamaros carried out the multiple kidnapping of the Brazilian consul, of Gordon Jones (who escaped on the same day) and of Dan Mitrione (who was later murdered)—on 31st July 1970.[3] A week later the Tupamaros kidnapped Dr. Claude Fly, who was also held, as was the Brazilian consul, until after Jackson himself was kidnapped.

For the next six months, Jackson became increasingly aware that he was being watched with a view to a kidnap. He observed that throughout daylight hours there was almost invariably a young student-aged 'family', father, mother and baby, picnicking in the park opposite his home. Though the characters changed, the pattern was too consistent to be mere chance. It became clear that this was part of a comprehensive study of his habits. He spotted a similar reconnaissance team observing the entrance to the Embassy—consisting of a boy and girl canoodling, but in such a way as to make it obvious that their attention was not on each other, but on him. Their scooter was parked nearby, and a check on its number plate by the Embassy security officer traced it to a university student of known terrorist affiliation. The scooter teams which regularly patrolled his Residence and

3. See Chapter 2.

the Embassy and shadowed his car in between showed even less discretion; though the boy and girl on the scooter changed, they regularly used the same scooter with the same number plate.

As the plan developed, the ambassador and his security officer noticed that there were regular 'dummy runs' by cars and trucks, cutting in on his official car at various points between his home and the Embassy, aiming to select a suitable site. There were other experiments evidently intended to practise cutting in between his car and the escort vehicle behind it. In these cars he began to recognize faces, and he was to see these faces again at, and after his kidnap.

The British Embassy was in the old business centre of Montevideo where the streets were extremely narrow and congested, so that a get-away after a kidnap would be extraordinarily difficult. The ambassador judged that a kidnap attempt would be unlikely there, but far likelier on the wide and often empty streets in the suburbs. He therefore developed a series of alternative routes through these suburbs, and varied his timings, so that the Tupamaros realized that it would be very difficult to catch him anywhere outside the old city. In the event, therefore, they planned their kidnap in the most difficult place, in the congested old city, close to the Embassy because this was the one place through which he had no choice but to travel.

This decision involved the Tupamaros in an elaborately co-ordinated operation which was extremely expensive in manpower and vehicles. For they realized that they would have to simultaneously block every junction on the periphery of a large area surrounding the point of attack to ensure that their get-away route would not be obstructed. This, in the event, they did.

For the actual kidnapping they selected a day just after the president had left for a seaside holiday, when a large part of the security forces had moved out of Montevideo to protect his route and his destination. They picked a particularly narrow street in which trucks were regularly parked on both sides to unload at wayside stores and where delays were not unusual. A large red van pulled out suddenly and barged into the ambassador's car, crushing its wing. The chauffeur got out to take particulars of the 'accident'. A man struck him down and another produced a machine gun from a basket of fruit and opened fire, wounding two of the ambassador's escort (who were, by his decision, not armed). One terrorist jumped into the driver's seat through the open door, unlocking the other doors from the inside. Three others got in, two of them administering a 'pistol whipping' to the ambassador as they drove off—apparently well conversant with the idiosyncracies of the Embassy Daimler—its door locks, its gear shift and its power steering.

Their elaborate traffic control plan gave them their clear get-away into a long, straight, empty street, five minutes out of town, where the ambassador was transferred to a waiting van. He feigned a swoon in the hope that he might be able to make a break whilst being carried to the van, but he had no chance. Before the van doors closed he heard the voice of an old lady asking if she could help, but he decided that 'to exploit the cover offered by one nice old lady would do her no good and me still less', so he resigned himself to captivity as the van doors slammed shut.

THE DIFFICULTIES OF THE ENEMY

Field-Marshal Wavell used to say that it is a common mistake to underestimate the difficulties of your enemy. Though protection of an individual from kidnapping is a daunting task, there are many things which can go wrong for the kidnapper. If the potential victim takes sensible precautions, these difficulties may well deter the kidnapper and lead him to divert his attack to an easier or less alert victim.

In the case of Sir Geoffrey Jackson (he was knighted by the Queen on his return to the U.K.) these precautions undoubtedly drove the Tupamaros into a far more comprehensive operation than usual. In fact, they might well have changed their target, but for their strong political reasons for picking a British victim at that time.

If the potential victim can spot and report the kind of recon-naissance and surveillance effort Sir Geoffrey has described, it should be possible for the government to counter them and probably to break up the attempt by making arrests. Why the Uruguayan Government in 1970–71 was unable to do this must remain a mystery. It may be that the size of the Tupamaros deployment nation-wide made it impracticable to follow up all such clues. They were then at their peak, about 3,000 strong—mainly intelligent students with time on their hands, a comfortable base to fall back on, and no shortage of money. Such a movement—and still more so a movement as rich as the ERP—also has great potential for corruption.

Be that as it may, there is little doubt that the kind of preparations needed for a major kidnapping attempt are such that an alert potential victim, and those responsible for his personal security, should almost certainly sense that something is afoot.

PHYSICAL PROTECTION

Bodyguards cannot give guaranteed protection as the terrorists will usually have the ability to concentrate enough strength to divert or overcome them. With the exception of the private armies of 40 or more men which vulnerable public figures used to employ in the Philippines, it is unlikely that any individual, and especially an executive of a commercial firm, will be protected by more than one or two bodyguards, or four at most. Their function is mainly to deter the attempt by increasing the risk of failure or capture. They can best do this if they are in at least two cars, in addition to the target car, both of which should be unobtrusive, one travelling some distance behind—but this too will often be precluded on grounds of economy. The terrorists may be able to pick any one of a hundred or even a thousand suitable victims, and they can hardly all be guarded in this way—unless they move in convoys, as discussed in the next chapter.

Bullet-proof cars with locked doors also increase the kidnappers' difficulties. They can use mines or armour-piercing weapons, but this may prejudice the prospects of capturing the victim alive—an essential part of a ransom-seeking operation. Moreover, it is not too difficult to devise a ruse for inducing the driver to open the door, as was done in Sir Geoffrey Jackson's case.

A good radio network—ideally with one of the sets in a car well-separated from the others—is an important precaution, but is useless unless backed up by a reliable control system and a police force geared for immediate response. An important element of a good police framework—which can make a city seem like a minefield to a terrorist—is the ability to snap a road block on every exit from the site of an incident within a few minutes. It may not be so difficult to find the money for this, as it is a measure as effective against bank-robbers as against kidnappers. It may, however, be part of the terrorists' tactics, not only to divert the government's resources in this way from social expenditure which benefits the community, but also by repeated false alarms to cause the public to be harassed by road blocks, checks and searches.

An often recommended technical aid is the miniature transmitter concealed in a belt or a shoe or even swallowed. There are larger, and therefore cheaper and more powerful transmitters, which can be carried in the car or in a briefcase. Such transmitters—of all sizes—do exist, but the receipt of their signals may be restricted by buildings to a very short range within a city. This can be overcome by using aircraft, but it will not be easy to have an aircraft airborne in time to be over the right area before the victim has left it. Another way is for the transmitter to emit a strident signal which interferes on every wavelength on every radio in the vicinity. There are many practical difficulties, not least of which is the price—for a system incorporating miniature sets and an effective control network is unlikely to cost less than $10,000 in all.

Nevertheless, the fear of such devices is always in the minds of kidnappers, and Sir Geoffrey Jackson was amused to hear his captors tearing apart the handle of his briefcase in their search for the non-existent radio beacon!

Tactical Precautions

Common sense and co-operation with the police count quite as much, if not more, than hardware, in dealing with kidnappers.

The first rule is to avoid routine as much as possible. It is not easy to get away from traditional working hours, and there may be little choice of routes in the immediate vicinity of the home and of the place of work. A useful stratagem is to use different cars and to avoid easily recognizable ones—though this may conflict with a desire to use a bullet-proofed vehicle.

Nevertheless, unless one has the scale of bodyguards and out-riders normally reserved for presidents of unstable republics, the other extreme—maximum unobtrusiveness—may often be safer than ostentatious, but inadequate protection.

The most important principle of all, however, is to co-operate fully with the police and to establish mutual confidence with them. If the police are themselves corrupt then no other precautions will be effective in any case. Assuming that they are honest, how-ever, their task can be made much easier if potential kidnap victims fall in with their plans, and especially if they pass on relevant information and sensible suspicions to the police intelli-gence authorities.

It needs moral courage to overcome the reluctance to make a fuss. Early in January 1971 Geoffrey Jackson was chided by an important visitor for 'seeing a Tupamaros behind every tree'. Two or three days later, he was their prisoner.

If the threat is serious enough, it may prove necessary to take more drastic action to defend both residence and movement, and this will be discussed in the next chapter. The point is, that there is always a solution, so long as the terrorists do not become so powerful that they can overthrow civilized government altogether. How far up the scale of defence one is prepared to go, depends on the price one is prepared to pay.

Chapter Five

Security at Home And at Work

A STATE OF SIEGE

TACTICAL precautions at home and at work are as important as in driving between the two.

Embassies, factories and offices are easier to guard than homes because one perimeter encloses many vulnerable people. This is borne out by the very small proportion of kidnaps of people from inside their place of work.

Where the threat verges on a state of war, it may be necessary for diplomats, officials and vulnerable business executives to move into houses in defended compounds. There is nothing new or even prohibitively difficult about this. It has frequently been a matter of course—for example, in the early settlements in America. The essential feature of this situation is the existence of a hostile and aggressive section of the population, or of a violent and clandestine gang or group of gangs which are dedicated to killing or terrorizing members of another section of the population; gangs which claim that they are justified in doing so, and which prove able to continue to do so on an unacceptable scale in defiance of the law and despite the efforts of law enforcement agencies to prevent them. Such a situation undoubtedly existed in Argentina in 1973–74. It also existed in 1971 in Uruguay, but since 1972 the Uruguayan Government has succeeded, by ruthless action, in establishing a law enforcement agency which can contain it. If the ERP and its satellites should succeed in rebuilding the threat to unacceptable proportions in Uruguay or in Bolivia or Chile—as its declared intention states—the same 'state of siege' might again become necessary in those countries. It is not without significance that *State of Siege* was the title of a bitter and nostalgic film about the Tupamaros in 1970 (intended to justify the killing of Dan Mitrione) which was made in Allende's Chile in 1972–73.

Historically, this 'state of siege' has not only applied to colonists or to expatriates or to the rich and important. Other and often quite poor sections of the population have had to group themselves into defended compounds for safe residence in the face of gangs of criminals or outlaws or simply of a hostile or lawless population. About forty Oxford and Cambridge Colleges, built in mediaeval times, are designed as fortresses, each for several hundred resident scholars. Ghettos—like the Montefiore quarter just outside the walls of the Old City of Jerusalem—provided for centuries a similar refuge for Jews amongst an Arab population. On a more spacious scale, housing settlements in some of the oil states are concentrated within defended perimeters.

It is a matter for consultation between host governments, diplomats and international corporations whether this degree of concentration and protection is necessary as the price to be paid for the continuance of diplomatic representation or of commercial operations. If they agree that defended residential compounds are necessary, then it can always be left to individual officials or executives to decide whether they (and their families) wish to live inside, or whether they wish to take their chance outside these compounds. And it is their decision whether their movement between these compounds and their places of work should be in convoys with escorts strong enough to master or deter the kind of attack which their enemies are capable of mounting. This may be cheaper in the end, both for host governments and for their guests, than trying to protect individuals ranging free.

This does not, however, offer a solution for the indigenous people who are targets for attack. In Argentina in 1974 there was a growing epidemic of political assassinations—of Argentine ministers, officials, executives, newspaper editors etc.—by left- and right-wing terrorist groups. Ultimately, that kind of situation can normally result only in a military government.

ISOLATION

The heaviest part of the price to be paid for living in a 'state of siege' may be the isolation of the official or executive, and of his family, from the local community.

This may be particularly serious for a diplomat and, if he comes from a country which the terrorists seem unlikely to want to embarrass, he may well decide that the price of isolation is not justified.

FAMILIES

Isolation of the family—whether in a defended compound or by voluntary curtailment of their activities while living freely—may also be necessary, but it could so inhibit their way of life that their presence would not be worthwhile. Much will depend on both the father and the family. A man in the front line of this modern form of warfare may decide that his family is as much out of place there as on the battlefield of a more conventional war or in a warship. Soldiers and sailors have long accepted this as part of their way of life. Some diplomats and executives may have to do so too.

If families are prepared to take the risk of being there, and the head of the family is prepared to let them do so, then certain voluntary precautions will be necessary, both because the abduction of wives and children is a well-established form of blackmail, and also because families are a common target for agents surreptitiously seeking information.

Wives must avoid ostentation—and especially avoid flamboyant and easily recognizable cars; they must do their best to merge with the landscape and with its fauna; and they must be careful in their choice of friends.

Children in their teens and early twenties are especially vulnerable. Their abduction attracts less odium than that of younger children. They are likely to know and understand more of what their father does. Since terrorist movements are largely led and manned by students or young graduates, children of this age are especially vulnerable to the calculated cultivation of their sympathy for the young or for the oppressed, or to an appeal to their spirit of adventure. It may be unwise in some countries for them to enrol in local universities—though this may depend much on their own character and on their relationship with their parents. The same considerations apply to their choice of friends and it is important for the parents at least to be aware of who these friends are. At the lowest end of the scale, a son or daughter may quite unconsciously be used as a source of information about his parents' habits and movements.

SECURITY OF BUILDINGS AND PERIMETERS

Even a private residence can be made into a fortress, at a price. Chinese millionaires in Singapore and Hong Kong have done this for generations against kidnapping by criminals or secret societies for ransom or blackmail. Professor C. Northcote Parkinson, in *Parkinson's Law*,[1] has described how they make the jump in a single bound from an unobtrusive palm-thatched hut to 'a well-fenced house guarded by an Alsatian hound. It is this move which has been termed "breaking the Hound Barrier".' A true word spoken in jest.

There are now many security firms and consultants who are prepared to survey the homes or offices of clients and to study their way of life in order to advise them on a plan for the security of themselves and their families. This advice will cover their habits and movements, the location and design of buildings, a scale of security guards or dogs, and the installation of security hardware.

A wide scale of security hardware is now available. It can be used for residences, offices, factories and their perimeters. It saves manpower, but costs money, and these must be balanced in the equation with the threat.

Fixed barriers, fences, locks and *lights* need little explanation. They can be supplemented to save manpower with many of the forms of detectors—of movement, vibration, heat, tampering etc.— described below. It may also be necessary in working premises to use special forms of locks which conform with regulations for

1. (London, John Murray, 1957).

unimpeded escape by staff in case of fire, while at the same time preventing unauthorized entry from outside.

A more sophisticated additional safeguard is the *electromagnetic interrogator* which may be used to check the fingerprints of a person seeking entry and to match these either to a card carried by him, or to a record of his prints in a data bank incorporated in the system. A lock will be automatically released only if they match correctly. (Holders of car park season tickets may be familiar with this system using simpler data than fingerprints.)

Space detectors are designed to detect body movements within a designated area. The simplest are *ultrasonic transceivers*, which transmit and receive sound waves of frequencies too high for the human ear to hear. They normally cover an egg-shaped volume of space about thirty feet by twenty feet and have the added advantage that, with careful siting, the waves can be reflected into otherwise concealed corners. Bodies entering the space reflect the waves, in the same way as aircraft reflect radar waves. To avoid extraneous signals from causing false alarms (e.g. the inaudible overtones from bells or other noises in a factory) it is normal for the alarm to be activated only if the body is moving— that is by the 'Doppler Effect'. This is the effect which gives the siren on an approaching car a higher note than when it is receding. Thus an ultrasonic transceiver should only activate the alarm if the range of the object is changing, so that the frequency of the reflected wave is a changing and not a steady one. Large numbers of transceivers can be linked to a single control unit which sounds the alarm—either in the building or in the local police station, or both. The transceivers and the control unit can be operated both by mains and battery to counter power-cuts or the cutting of cables.

Radar or *micro-wave* systems operate in the same way, but can operate at much longer ranges. A radar beam can cover a volume of several million cubic feet inside a building or can be directed at long range on outside gates or along fences.

Photo-electric detectors are familiar to anyone who has passed through an automatic door into an airport terminal. The body interrupts a beam of light directed across the entrance on to a photo-electric cell. The alarm system can be operated in the same ways as for other forms of space detection.

Closed-circuit television for surveillance or detection of movement is sufficiently familiar to need no further explanation. *Surveillance cameras* can also be activated automatically to provide photographic evidence of the intruder.

There are other forms of *body detection* as well as those which detect movement in space.

Weight detectors are the simplest. These normally consist of *pressure mats* across doorways or passages which close an electrical circuit when someone steps on them. Ideally they should be large enough not to be jumped over, but smaller ones have the advantage that people who live or work in the house or building can stride across them, enabling them to be kept switched on (especially at times when authorized movement may only be occasional, such as from a bedroom to a bathroom at night).

Infra-red detectors are operated by the heat of the body. They have the advantage of a very wide field of view and normally operate up to about thirty feet in range. Other forms of heat—of, for example, a vehicle engine—can be detected at much longer ranges, but the longer the range, the greater the risk of false alarms. *Image-intensifiers* can be used to monitor movement or intrusion in the dark.

Vibration or *seismic detectors* can detect, electronically or magnetically, vibrations caused by a wide variety of intrusive activities, including body movements on floors, hammering, drilling, digging, blasting, tunnelling or almost any form of impact or vibration to which they may be tuned.

Finally there are numerous *anti tampering* devices, which include the *vibration* or *seismic detectors* mentioned above.

There is a large range of *proximity detectors* which are activated by touching, for example, a bolt, handle or window catch. These can be activated by pressure, or by pulling an attached wire (the loop alarm), either of which will close an electric circuit and operate the alarm. More sensitive trip mechanisms can include a magnetic reed, or a magnet which, when moved, repels another magnet into closing an electric circuit. The closure or interruption of an electric circuit may be combined with some already built-in device, just as a courtesy light is operated by opening the door of a car. This same current can operate an intrusion alarm which can be switched off by an authorized user possessing a key.

Other anti-tampering devices can be operated by *impact*—if, for example, a glass window or door is forcibly broken.

HARDWARE AND HUMAN BEINGS

No hardware can rival a human being, with ears, eyes and a brain, and with the judgement to take action. Hardware, however, may be cheaper and enables one human brain to cover more ground.

Similarly, neither hardware nor security guards can overcome stupidity, carelessness or recklessness by the people using the building, and especially by those who may be the personal targets for attack. The degree of inconvenience and self-discipline to be tolerated must be balanced against the degree of risk to be accepted, but a manifestation of conscientious and disciplined protection is likely to be an effective deterrent in itself and will often induce the terrorist to transfer his attention to softer targets.

Chapter Six

The Prisoner's Dilemma

PEOPLE'S PRISON

'STUDENTS' Prison' would be a more accurate description than 'People's Prison'. Terrorist movements seldom have more than very small minority support from the people and—with the exception of the IRA, who do not have 'people's prisons'— virtually no support from the working classes for whom they usually claim to speak. Even in the most sympathetic apologia for them—such as Maria Esther Gilio's *The Tupamaros*[1]—the picture which emerges is one of earnest young intellectuals increasingly frustrated by their lack of response from the ordinary people. And out of roughly thirty Tupamaros who took turns to guard Geoffrey Jackson in his eight months in a 'people's prison', only one was identifiably a manual worker. All the others were apparently university students or ex-students.

Urban terrorists most often hold their prisoners in cellars in relatively prosperous suburbs where—as middle-class students— they can come and go between their public life and their clandestine life without looking out of place. The entrance to the cellar will almost invariably be from a garage or small warehouse in which a van carrying a prisoner—or anyone else—can unload out of sight. It will often be located in a small factory or workshop, which may operate also in its proper role in order not to excite suspicion. The cellar itself will usually be very small.

This pattern is not, of course, invariable. Since being depicted in the film *State of Siege*, holding a prisoner in a tent in a *bourgeois* drawing-room has become popular. There is no reason why a prisoner should not be held in a shack in a shanty-town or

1. (London, Secker and Warburg, 1972).

in a mountain village or cave. This is, however, unusual as the inhabitants of such areas have little time for intellectual terrorists, so their prisons are likely to be easier to detect, and probably also easier to surround and attack.

CONTINGENCY PLANNING

Since a potential victim will often have grounds for suspicion that he is on the terrorists' list—both from the pattern of events in the country and from indications that he is being watched—a certain amount of contingency planning may be both possible and wise.

Contingency planning with the local government and police will depend upon relationships with them and upon how sure the potential victim feels about whom he can trust. Sometimes, in these situations, a tacit 'live-and-let-live' arrangement is arrived at between the terrorists and the police, or with individual police officers, in which certain understandings are defined. It may, for example, be understood that in the event of the arrest of a terrorist one of the police officers in the radio control station will notify a particular lawyer who regularly acts for the movement, in exchange for which those officers who subscribe to the understanding are guaranteed immunity from personal attack. (The lawyer, as well as arranging for representation, will also be able to alert the headquarters of the movement.) From this relatively innocuous beginning, the understanding may go a great deal further, to the point where the police agree to give the terrorists free rein in certain areas, in exchange for the terrorists agreeing to keep out of others. The extreme stage is reached when the police force, as a whole, connives with a particular group, setting no limit to their activities other than that the group agrees not to 'kill the goose' by acting in such a way that the understanding becomes too obvious. In such a case, contingency planning with the police would be foolhardy and the problem of security is virtually insoluble.

Discussion of contingency plans by the potential victim with his own government or firm is most important. This should cover the policy to be adopted towards blackmail or ransom demands;

the question of whether an attack should be mounted on the hide-out if it is located; and the action to be taken over the victim's family and possessions. It may also be possible to agree on the use of certain code words or phrases in the event of the prisoner having the opportunity to send out taped or written messages.

ACTION AT THE TIME OF CAPTURE

The moment of an attempted kidnap may offer the victim the last opportunity to exercise boldness in trying to escape. This was well demonstrated by U.S. consul general Curtis S. Cutter in Porto Allegro, Brazil, on the evening of 5th April 1970—the day on which the body of the murdered German ambassador had been found in Guatemala. Cutter, with his wife and a friend, were driving home from a dinner engagement when a car blocked their path and four or five men armed with submachine guns jumped out. Cutter accelerated, knocking down one of the terrorists. The terrorists opened fire and wounded him, but Cutter drove on and escaped.

Otherwise, apart from taking any chance to let bystanders know his identity so that the hunt will start without delay, there is probably little that the victim can do, once he has been overpowered by well-organized kidnappers. They are unlikely to let him see where he is being taken.

INTERROGATION

Interrogation, both immediately after capture, and thereafter in depth, must be taken for granted, and the victim's only defence is to be physically and mentally prepared for it. A small number of British soldiers in units designed to operate behind enemy lines, and some others in jobs in which there is a particular risk of capture and interrogation, are put through an intensive exercise in which they are subjected to all known techniques of interrogation, other than actual physical torture. It might be thought that such an exercise would not be effective, as the victim knows that it is 'not for real'. This, however, is overcome in two ways; firstly the exercise is so designed that the victim knows that others who are in the role of being 'on the run' will be subjected to the same ordeal if he betrays them; and secondly, he knows that if he folds up easily he will be dismissed as unsuitable for the job and, apart from the humiliation, he will only have won his place in this *élite* unit against stiff competition and he will be strongly motivated to hold this place. All who have been subjected to this training testify to its effectiveness.

Physical torture is not as common or as effective as is supposed. The victim is likely to say what he thinks his interrogators want him to say and this may not be the truth. If the aim is to gain information, it will therefore be unreliable. If the aim is to extort a statement from a public figure for propaganda, it will carry little weight. Torture—whether by terrorists, soldiers or by policemen—is a sign of lack of confidence. It is significant that the most experienced professionals in the art of oppression, the Soviet KGB, have now largely abandoned physical torture.

Much more sophisticated and effective are the now well-established techniques of mental disorientation. These use the results of Pavlov's experiments on animals, in which kindness is alternated with brutality, and tension with reassurance, to confuse the victim. Eventually, his mental reactions and moral judgements may become so reversed that, for example, he believes it is right for him to speak and not be silent, or to betray and not to protect.

This process can be accentuated by various other techniques designed to induce a feeling of isolation and uneasiness. This is mainly achieved by a process known as 'sensory deprivation' in which the victim is subjected either to an unchanging sensory input—e.g. a steady continuous noise—or deprived of any sensory input at all, by being kept in total silence with his eyes covered or in a dark or featureless room. Another element is to deny the victim any sight of, or communication with, other human beings, so that he does not know where he is or what is happening. He sees no daylight so that he loses count of time, and his confusion is increased by irregular and inadequate meals and by denial of sleep.

Then there are drugs, such as scopolamine, designed to relax resistance and unleash his tongue. Some of these drugs rely on 'placebo' effects, based upon the victim's belief in the effectiveness of such drugs. Conscious of their relaxing effect he believes that it is useless for him to resist the impulse to speak freely, so he speaks.

It is possible for the victim to resist these drugs provided that he does know their limitations. Geoffrey Jackson was injected with drugs while bumping along in the van within minutes of his capture and again immediately on arrival in his prison. While they produced some light-headedness, he never felt wholly dominated by them. Being aware that he was drugged, he concentrated his mind on dividing his ideas into two categories: selecting unimportant ones on which he would be fluent to the point of verbosity, and others on which he would blur his answers, while at the same time trying to make them verbose enough so as to be indistinguishable from the important ones.[2]

Geoffrey Jackson also somewhat disarmed his captors from the start by retaining his sense of humour. He made them laugh when they were trying to inject him with a needle in the moving car by asking if they were trying to tattoo the Tupamaro emblem on the back of his hand. He continued to make them laugh on occasions throughout his captivity and this laughter drew out— at least from a few of them—some vestiges of humanity which survived inside the terrorist armour they had built around their personalities. We shall return to this subject in a later chapter.

It is easy to lay down instructions that a prisoner should maintain a cold, hard refusal to communicate with his captors. This depends on the individual. It may work for a time, and some men and women have endured and will maintain their silence to the death. In the face of the other techniques described, however, everyone will have a breaking point—which may eventually overtake the strongest of men, if his mind has been scientifically deranged. His only hope then, is for his mind to be so confused that what he says will be inaccurate and unintelligible, as it often is under torture. For some, it may be best to hold out and refuse to communicate at all, but many ordinary people may have to settle for trying to confuse the interrogator as much as he tries to

2. Jackson, *op. cit.* (pp. 39–40).

confuse his victim, so that it is impossible to detect when really important information is being deliberately obscured.

There is no real antidote to the loathsome techniques of modern interrogation—and they are equally loathsome which ever side uses them. The victim can only aim to hold on to that hard core of information whose revelation would place others in jeopardy and to try, by a balance of firmness and flexibility, to sustain his own health and sanity.

HEALTH—MENTAL AND PHYSICAL

Life in a cellar is devastatingly unhealthy. There are systems of indoor exercises—like the Canadian Air Force 5BX system—which can be done in a confined space and which are of proven value. As part of his contingency planning, a potential victim would do well to memorize and practise some such system, and to maintain himself in a good state of health in readiness to face the ordeal, if it comes.

The average victim, by nature of the office which makes him a target, is likely to be middle-aged and accustomed to reasonable home comforts and privacy. He may find it intensely humiliating to be cooped up in a cell the size of a cupboard, guarded and gratuitously insulted by teenagers, and forced to perform all his bodily functions in sordid conditions in their presence. He must be mentally prepared for this, and determined to do whatever can be done to maintain his self-respect and his physical and mental health, which are his most important capital.

Here again, an attempt at some kind of human contact with the jailers may pay dividends. In seeking this, he can reflect that they too are, in a sense, imprisoned in circumstances physically similar to his own; their share of the cellar may be no bigger than his. While they are not physically restrained by a cage, they are, however, restrained by their commitment to their party and by the knowledge that if they waver from it, their knowledge of party secrets will make their own lives inevitably forfeit. Some of them will have doubts, and these doubts will be increased if they give way, in their shared loneliness, to even a glimmer of warmth in their relationship with their prisoner. Whether or not this eventually contributes to their cure, it should certainly contribute to the mental health of the prisoner.

He must also be determined to keep his mind engaged. Many who were prisoners in World War II or in Korea have testified that the activity which kept them sane was constant planning for escape, however hopeless this may have seemed. Military training teaches soldiers that they will best protect their own health by adopting this attitude of mind from the start. A kidnap victim can do the same.

If his captors allow him books, pencils and paper he can also do much with these. If not, he can divert his mind by such stratagems as memorizing (or composing) verse, by devising stories or letters to be written later, or by maintaining and constantly repeating to himself a mental diary of events. This is healthier in every respect than keeping a written diary—even if given the opportunity to do so.

The prisoner's physical and mental health are vital; enabling him to endure interrogation (and similarly the rest of his ordeal), to seize any opportunity for escape and—ultimately—allowing him to readjust to a normal life after his release.

The longer-term influence he may have on his captors is less urgent, but this can in the end have a very significant effect on what is becoming a world problem—the cure of the disease called 'terrorism'. This is the subject of a later chapter.

III. BOMBS

Chapter Seven

Bombs and Fuses

TYPES OF BOMB

BOMBS are one of the oldest weapons of the political terrorist. Guy Fawkes tried to blow up the Houses of Parliament on 5th November 1605, and became the forerunner of those who did manage to set off a not dissimilar bomb there in 1974. The archetype of the nineteenth-century anarchist has an object like a cannon-ball concealed in his cloak with a telltale wisp of smoke coming out of the top. No early Western or melodrama in the 1920s was worth its salt without a sheriff or a heroine strapped to a barrel of dynamite with five feet of fuse fizzing on the floor.

Two world wars have, in this century, rationalized and streamlined the art of indirect killing. Mines were manufactured by the million in 1941–44, to be set off by the pressure of a tank track, by a man falling over a trip-wire, or by a concealed operator with an electric switch. Army engineers were taught to recognize these factory-made devices and to learn precisely how they worked. Once spotted, they could be neutralized with some confidence.

Those days have passed. The terrorist bomb of today is once again an improvised bomb, and it may take any of a hundred different forms. It is axiomatic that the bomb which a bomb-disposal man has to disarm will be different from any which he may have studied or examined. All the potential victim can do is to understand the principles of bomb mechanisms and how they are used, so that he can easily detect one, and can set about dealing with it logically. Unless he is a trained bomb-disposer, 'dealing with it' is best interpreted as leaving it alone, isolating it and calling for help.

The terrorist bomb may be posted in a letter or a parcel; it may be put in a shopping bag, with a time fuse, in a pub, a bus

75

station or in a tourist centre like the Tower of London, and be left to blow up indiscriminately whoever may be there. It may be left in a suitcase or carton in a station baggage room, in the luggage compartment of a bus or aircraft, or in a basement of a public building. It may be locked in the boot of a car; or it may simply be a booby-trap, to be set off by any simple action, such as opening a door or treading on a floorboard.

Incendiary bombs, though less lethal, are easier to place and can sometimes be made entirely of materials to be found inside a shop or warehouse. The problem of smuggling them in need not in this case arise.

It is surprising that more people are not killed by bombs, in view of the many different ways in which they can be planted. One encouraging fact, however, is that a very large proportion of the people preparing or planting bombs become their own victims. This has been particularly the case in Northern Ireland, where the IRA admitted that more of their men have been killed by their own bombs than by the army or the police.[1]

THE BASIC ELEMENTS OF A BOMB

A bomb consists of three fundamental elements: a *high explosive charge*, which may vary from a few ounces in a letter bomb to a hundred pounds or more in a car bomb. This charge is made of an inert explosive, which can be safely handled, dropped, cut or crushed. It can only be set off by a *detonator*, which normally consists of a small, steel tube about two inches long by a quarter of an inch diameter, containing a very small quantity of a supersensitive explosive, such as fulminate of mercury. So small is this detonator, that if it goes off on its own it will do no more than blow off a finger. Yet it is powerful enough to detonate the main explosive charge—sometimes aided by an intermediate charge or primer. The detonator will explode if crushed, but is generally set off by the heat of a flash. This flash is produced by initiating one of many types of *fuse*, either by firing a cap (as in a gun) or by chemical action, or by the passage of an electric current through

1. *Freedom Struggle by the Provisional IRA*, 1973.

a wire filament as in a light bulb. The flash of the fuse sets off the detonator, and the detonator sets off the main charge.

Methods of initiation can be subdivided into those which the victim sets off—that is, by *handling*; those which are set off by various forms of *time fuse*; and those which are set off by *remote control* or by *altitude*.

FUSES OPERATED BY HANDLING

A common type of *handling* fuse is the *release* mechanism, the most familiar kind being the hand grenade. A lever is held under pressure along the side of the bomb or grenade. When the lever is released, it flies up under pressure of a spring and releases a trigger mechanism which fires a hammer against a cap just as in the firing of a pistol. In the case of a hand grenade, this cap initiates a short time fuse, usually four-and-a-half or seven seconds, which allows the operator time to throw it through the air. In the case of a bomb, such as a parcel bomb or booby-trap, the release of the lever and the firing of the cap may detonate the explosive charge instantaneously. The lever is normally held in a safe position by a split pin. In the case of a grenade, the lever is grasped in the hand ready for throwing and the pin removed. Letting go of the grenade releases the lever. In the case of a bomb, the lever may be held by binding up a parcel, by closing the lid of a suitcase or cupboard door, or in any number of other ways, such as inserting the bomb, disguised as an ornament, in a cardboard tube. In all of these cases the split pin is usually fixed to a string so that it can be withdrawn when the operator is satisfied that the lever is safely imprisoned. The bomb is then live. It will be set off by undoing the binding of the parcel, by opening the suitcase or cupboard, or by removing the ornament from its cardboard tube.

Another kind of release fuse can be fired *electrically*, by allowing two electrical contacts to close a battery circuit and fire a detonator. But this is less commonly used in release fuses than in the other types described hereafter.

The next group of handling fuses are of the *pull* type, set off by the act of pulling as opposed to the act of releasing. The actual firing may be by mechanical or electrical means. The *mechanical* firing mechanism is a trigger, like the trigger of a gun. In a bomb it is generally more sensitive than a pistol trigger. It can comprise almost any kind of trip mechanism, operated by pulling a wire attached to the lid of a package or to a door, simply by pulling out a pin which has been holding back the firing-hammer.

The *electrical* type of pull fuse is particularly common in letter or parcel bombs. It consists of a simple battery and electrical circuit which, when closed, forms a current which heats the filament in an electric detonator, which in turn fires the charge. A very easy way of closing the circuit is to attach the wires to pieces of tinfoil fixed on to the two inside faces of a clothes peg. These are kept apart by a splinter of wood attached to whatever is intended to set off the bomb—e.g. to the lid of a box. When the splinter is pulled out, the clothes peg springs shut, closing the circuit. In another method, often used in letter bombs or in bombs concealed in books sent by post, the two pieces of tinfoil are fixed on to two facing pages. They are kept apart by a piece of card fixed to the bottom of the envelope. When the letter or book is pulled out of the envelope the card stays behind allowing the pages to touch and closing the circuit.

Pressure is another way of firing a fuse. In its crudest form this could be done simply by placing the detonator itself, resting on its main charge, under a loose floorboard so that the weight of a man would crush it. This, however, is not very reliable, highly dangerous to set up, and therefore very rare. Normally, pressure fuses are set off mechanically, electrically or chemically.

The *mechanical* pressure fuse follows the same principle as the release and pull mechanism, and can be compared to the pressure of a finger on a trigger. It can be operated by tripping and releasing a spring hammer, or by the pressure shearing a pin which is holding back the hammer. A mechanical pressure switch is most commonly used for booby-traps under a mat or a loose floorboard.

The *electrical* pressure fuse again follows the same principle as the electrical pull fuse, except that the electrical contact is made by squeezing and not by pulling. The squeeze may simply deflect or compress a spring holding two contacts apart—which is precisely how a bell-push works; or the squeeze may cause some weak separator—like a match-box—to collapse and thus allow the contacts to come together.

Pressure fuses can also be operated by the *chemical* method. In its crudest form the flash can simply be caused by friction on a match composition, exactly like striking a match, but this is unreliable and therefore rare. More commonly, the pressure crushes a glass phial containing a chemical which causes a flash when it comes into contact with another chemical.

There are other forms of *electrical firing* which do not fall into any of the above categories. Instead of a chemical, for example, a phial may contain water which closes an electrical circuit when the phial is broken. An electrical contact may be closed by a *tilting* motion, which causes, for example, a steel ball to roll into a gap, or a pendulum to swing against a metal contact. This method is extremely sensitive, and has been used as an anti-handling device in a suitcase bomb. The circuit is kept switched off altogether while the suitcase is transported and dumped and then, when the operator is quite sure that it is balanced correctly and that he will not be moving it again, he switches on the rest of the circuit, leaving it ready to be closed by the tilt.

Also amongst the handling type are the *photo-electric* fuses. These are usually designed to catch the bomb-disposal man when he comes along to deal with the bomb. The detonator is fired by the electric current from a photo-electric cell activated when light is played on it. This could be used in a bomb placed in a dark cupboard, which would therefore fire when the opening of the door allows the light to enter. Alternatively the bomb may be designed to be fired when torch-light is played on it. This method was used in Hong Kong in 1967 when a fairly obvious bomb was placed in a dark street. It went off wounding a soldier when he shone his torch on it. It only worked once, as the soldiers thereafter were ready for it.

X-ray sensitive fuses are a recent development, designed to thwart X-ray detection machines for letter, parcel or suitcase bombs.

TIME FUSES

The next group of fuses are *time fuses*, which are often used in conjunction with handling fuses, so that, for example, the bomb will either go off if the boot of a car is opened or after a specified number of minutes have elapsed, whichever comes first.

Time fuses are most commonly operated by a *clock* mechanism which closes and fires an electrical circuit. A simple way is to connect one wire to the metal hand of a watch or clock and to connect the other to an insulated metal pin which projects from the face of the clock beside the time at which the bomb is to fire. If the time required is measured in minutes, the minute-hand is used. If it is more than an hour, the hour-hand will be used and the minute-hand is removed altogether.

Time fuses can also be *chemical*. In this case, there is a bare metal wire holding the spring of a firing mechanism under tension. This wire is inside a plastic tube which also contains a glass phial of acid. When the operator wishes to set the delay fuse in motion he squeezes the plastic tube until the phial inside breaks and the acid is released coming into contact with the bare wire. The acid and the wire are so designed that after a specified time—which may be anything from an hour to three days or more—the acid will eat through the wire and release the spring, firing the bomb.

ALTITUDE FUSES

A unique type of fuse is the *altitude fuse* which is operated when the atmospheric pressure falls below a certain level. This is used to set off a bomb in an aircraft when it reaches a high altitude.

REMOTE CONTROL FUSES

The third type of fuse is operated by *remote control* by a man watching from a concealed position.

The simplest method is an *electrical* circuit connected to a bell-push which the operator presses when his victim walks up to the bomb, or when a vehicle passes a particular point on the road. This last is called a *fougasse*. It may, for example, be concealed in a milestone or grassy bank, and is set off by a man overlooking the road from an embankment.

The wires, however, may give this away—not so much on a country road as in a built-up area. In this case the operator may use a *radio-control* system, of the type which can be bought in a toyshop for controlling model aircraft or toy boats.

Chapter Eight

Recognition and Detection

WHAT CAN BE DETECTED

VIRTUALLY every bomb contains metal. Detonators are in a metal tube. Firing pins and springs are made of metal. Electric wires are made of metal. Metal can be detected by electronic mine detectors; it also shows up clearly in an X-ray photograph—and the shapes are usually characteristic.

Explosives can also be 'sniffed' by electrochemical devices and by specially trained dogs.

More effective than any of these, however, are the signs that indicate something unusual—the feel of a letter, the parking of a car, or its number plates, or the suspicious behaviour of a man with a shopping bag or suitcase. It does not require special skill or equipment to recognize such things, just alertness and an awareness of what to look for. This awareness probably saves more lives than all the detection equipment put together.

LETTER BOMBS

A letter bomb is likely to be at least a quarter, and more probably, half an inch thick—so it will feel like a paper-back book or perhaps a folded report or pamphlet, rather than a simple letter. It will, however, probably feel heavier than if it contained the same thickness of paper. The explosive may 'sweat', causing greasy marks, and there may be a smell of marzipan. The package will also bend in a different way, either giving a suspicious feeling of rigidity or an equally suspicious feeling of lack of elasticity—in other words, it may have the 'dead' feeling of putty or clay, rather than the springy feeling of a pamphlet or a sheaf of papers. A suspicious package should obviously not be bent too violently,

82

but it will have been designed to survive normal handling in the mail so it will not be so very delicate.

The envelope and its address may also give ground for suspicion. Typed addresses are likely to lack the professional touch of a secretary who types every day. It is, however, a mistake to assume the addresses will be mis-spelt and crudely written. Since most terrorists are students or graduates and come from middle-class backgrounds, they not only have cultured handwriting, but may be familiar with the trivia of etiquette and forms of address. A letter bomb addressed in 1973 to Lieutenant-General Sir John Sharp at the Ministry of Defence in London had every one of his decorations and every comma and bracket in his rather complicated departmental address meticulously correct. Handwriting experts testified that it had probably been written by a female with university education.

Nevertheless a potential victim, even with a voluminous mail, will often be able to sense which packages, if any, are suspicious. First, he will rule out any which are too small or too light to contain bombs; then he will try to recognize what the others are, who sent them and why. Fortunately most letters containing books, pamphlets or reports carry some indication of the sender, and few are mysterious.

The chances are that an envelope containing a bomb will have other unusual features. If, for example, it is designed to fire when the contents are pulled out of the top, they may well have been inserted from the side, and the side flap of the envelope will in that case not look quite the same as when it came from the factory. There may be a hole through which a split pin or other safety device has been pulled out with a wire. The envelope will have signs of more than usual fingering. There may be an unusual smell. All of these facts add up to a hunch that something is odd, and this should be enough to induce the victim or his secretary to put the package aside for more professional examination— initially by an X-ray machine.

A large office may have its own X-ray machine. These are very efficient and quick to use but expensive to buy, so most people will need to ask the police to do the X-ray test. The police are also better equipped to deal with X-ray sensitive fuses if these are incorporated as booby-traps.

PARCEL BOMBS

Parcel bombs are less easy to recognize than letter bombs, because there are so many ways in which a parcel may be wrapped without suspicion. There is also much more scope for concealing and padding the explosives, detonators and firing mechanisms.

The first question to ask will be 'who sent this, and why?' Parcels nearly always come either from friends whose handwriting is known, or from offices which indicate who they are. In other cases a recipient under threat will be wise to refer a parcel for X-ray testing.

With parcels, more than letters, suspicion is quite likely to be aroused during the process of removing the wrapping—again by something unusual. There may, for example, be a superfluous second wrapping inside, probably with a hole from which a safety device was removed before the final outside wrapping was added. There may be something strange about the weight, the balance, the sound or the smell. If the recipient constantly asks himself 'what is this? who sent it? and why?' it is unlikely that he will fail to notice something odd before it is too late.

A skilled parcel bomber will, of course, be aware of all these things and will do his best to allay suspicion. Fortunately, however, more parcel bombs and letter bombs are detected and disposed of, than are detonated.

SHOPPING BAG BOMBS

On 17th July 1974 terrorists, believed to be from the IRA, planted a time bomb in a shopping bag in the armoury of the Tower of London—a tourist centre particularly attractive to children interested in the mediaeval suits of armour it contains. No warning was given. One woman was killed and 41 other people were injured, most of them children, and most of them visitors from overseas.

On 21st November 1974, twenty people were killed when terrorists placed bombs in two crowded pubs in the centre of Birmingham. During the previous few weeks, there had been bombs in pubs in Guildford and Woolwich which were close to military barracks but there were no barracks near the pubs selected in Birmingham. It was pay night for wage-earners in the factories and offices and most of the twenty killed were young workers and their friends. Another 180 were injured.

There is no practicable defence against this kind of attack. Many thousands of tourists enter the Tower of London every day during the summer, many of them carrying shopping bags, picnic lunches, handbags or top-coats any of which could contain a bomb. The same goes for almost any pub in the country. To search every visitor to the Tower of London and everyone going into a pub for a drink is hardly conceivable, nor is there any particular reason for choosing those targets rather than, say for example, railway stations, bus stations or supermarkets, all of which have been selected as targets in Northern Ireland. These attacks are indiscriminate ones directed at the community as a whole. They have almost always been counter productive, both in England and in Northern Ireland. So it proved on 'Bloody Friday' on 21st July 1972 when the IRA set off 19 bombs in bus stations and shopping streets during a peak shopping hour in Belfast.[1] The principal victims, predictably, were mothers and children, and 'Bloody Friday' led to counter measures which were made possible only by the mood of public revulsion against the IRA even in areas of Belfast and Londonderry where they normally enjoyed their most loyal support. The Irish community in Britain was equally revolted by the Birmingham bombs and there was overwhelming public approval for the banning of the IRA and the tougher laws against terrorism passed in Parliament a few days later.

The almost universal revulsion is in fact the only antidote—it can never be more than that—to this particularly mean and indiscriminate form of attack. The revulsion can also lead to a greater public alertness and readiness to help the police. A good example of this was at Baker Street Station in 1973, where there already had been a previous bomb. The terrorist placed a shopping bag

1. See Richard Clutterbuck, *Protest and the Urban Guerrilla* (London, Cassell, 1973–0, p. 132, and New York, Abelard-Schuman, 1974, p. 140).

containing a second bomb on the bridge above the two crowded platforms. An alert railwayman though it looked odd. Someone might absentmindedly put down a shopping bag beside a ticket machine but why on a bridge? He called the police and the bomb was defused.

After the Birmingham bombs the public was similarly on the lookout for suspicious packages, for people behaving strangely and, above all, for the 'safe houses' from which terrorists operate. The very small number of people in Britain who supported the IRA found themselves more closely watched and more positively reported by their neighbours if they acted suspiciously.

Suitcase Bombs

The suitcase bomb is the big brother of the shopping bag bomb and its natural habitat is obviously in the world of travel—in aircraft, buses and trains and in their terminals and baggage rooms.

On 21st February 1970 a Swiss airliner blew up in mid-air killing all 55 passengers and crew. This was caused by a suitcase bomb placed by a small breakaway group from the Popular Front for the Liberation of Palestine which called itself the PFLP General Command. It was almost certainly detonated by an altitude fuse. A similar bomb exploded in an Austrian airliner on the same day, but the pilot managed to make a safe landing.

On 23rd July 1974 an airliner carrying 92 passengers and crew from Belfast to London made an emergency landing in Manchester after an IRA telephone warning ten minutes after take-off saying that there was a bomb on board. The bomb was found in a bag under one of the seats. The timing mechanism had fired, but had failed to detonate the charge. If it had, all 92 people could have been killed. The reason they chose that particular aircraft was no doubt because it was carrying two policemen to London to receive gallantry awards from the Queen, accompanied by Mr. James Flanagan, the Chief Constable of Northern Ireland, who is a Catholic and therefore a particular target for the IRA. The fact that they were prepared to kill 89 other people indiscriminately at the same time tells its own story.

The same is true of a suitcase bomb placed on 3rd February

1974 in the luggage compartment of a bus which was known often to carry service men and their families back to Catterick Camp after they had visited their parents and grandparents in Manchester. Twelve people were killed, including a complete family: father, mother and their children aged five and two.

Other suitcase bombs have gone off in railway stations and other places frequented by people in no way concerned with the terrorists' war. This is another counter-productive weapon used by the IRA. In the case of suitcase bombs in aircraft, these should normally be detected by the measures described in the following chapters, used to guard against hijacking. Suitcases loaded into buses and trains may excite suspicion if those who load them do not travel themselves. This does not, obviously, apply to suitcases checked into luggage rooms, and in all cases there is a particular hazard from anti-handling devices. Generally, as for the shopping bag bomb, the only antidote is the reaction of public fury and hence of public alertness. This is the alertness needed in spotting anything unusual about the suitcase, about how and where it is placed, and in the behaviour of those who place it. Nevertheless, innocent people in crowded public places or public transport are the easiest of all targets for the terrorists to attack and the most difficult to guard.

CAR BOMBS

The car bomb, again, is closely related to the shopping bag and suitcase bombs and is generally initiated by the same kinds of time fuse—with a stronger likelihood of an anti-handling fuse being incorporated as well, operated by opening the car door or boot or switching on the ignition.

The car bomb is commonly used to attack property, such as factories, shops or government buildings and it is quite usual for the terrorists to telephone a warning some twenty minutes in advance in order to avoid the adverse propaganda which would result from the slaughter of large numbers of innocent people. This prospect does seem to daunt the terrorist more than it does in the case of other types of bombs because a car bomb often contains 50 or 100 lb. of explosive as compared with a normal charge of under 5 lb. in a shopping bag and 10 lb. in a suitcase.

Because of the problems of acquiring such large quantities of bulk explosives without arousing suspicion, it has become increasingly common for car bombers to use an improvised explosive which can be made by mixing an easily obtainable chemical fertilizer with diesel oil. This explosive is very inert and requires a priming charge (of one or two sticks of gelignite or equivalent) in addition to the normal detonator and fuse.

The charge is most easily concealed in a sack or suitcase in the boot of the car, and if this is locked after the timing mechanism is set in motion, there is no reliable means of detection, since the metal body of the car will hamper the use of X-rays or metal detectors and a reasonably tight boot, in the open air, is unlikely to release enough vapour from the explosive to be spotted by a chemical sniffer or by a trained dog.

Unless the operator is stupid enough to leave visible wires, detection must therefore rely on the origins, movement and parking of the car. Various remotely controlled devices have now been developed for investigating suspicious cars, blowing open locked boots and, if necessary, blowing up the car itself after the area has been cleared and precautions taken against fire.

In obvious targets for attack, such as barracks or outside government buildings, it is practicable to ban parking within destructive range, and this has now been extended to many shopping streets in the centre of Belfast and other Northern Irish towns. Factories may be difficult to defend—and they are often targets for attack, on the overt grounds of attacking capitalist society but with the indirect aim of increasing unemployment, as commended by Carlos Marighela.

Car bombs, though there is no sure defence against them, are in one respect easier to detect than other types of bomb. Whereas all the ingredients for a shopping bag bomb can be carried without suspicion into a small room behind a shop or into a block of flats and assembled there, the ingredients for a car bomb are more bulky, and have probably to be assembled in a garage or warehouse. They must also be acquired from many different sources: large bags of fertilizer or drums of diesel fuel may not fit the usual life-style of the terrorists, so are more likely to arouse the suspicion of neighbours. Alternatively, the theft or smuggling of large quantities of commercial explosives from mines or quarries takes considerable organization unless precautions there are exceptionally lax. Detonators may have to be found from yet another source as they are usually subject to particularly strict accounting and control.

A combination of a time fuse and an anti-handling fuse requires considerable expertise and the technical expert who assembles them is likely to be too valuable a man to put at risk in driving and parking the car in the target area. While the car is being parked, yet another man has to telephone a warning in order to avoid counter-productive casualties, and this has to be done a precise number of minutes—usually 15 or 20—before the fuse is timed to fire.

All of this requires a great deal of co-ordination—which is not always the strong suit of guerrilla movements dedicated to 'spontaneity'. Things often go wrong—as, for example, when the IRA telephoned a warning that a bomb would go off in a certain street in Belfast. The police quickly cleared the crowds into the next street—only for the bomb to explode in their faces in the very street in which they were taking refuge. Widely interpreted as diabolically cunning, this was almost certainly a case in which the driver of the bomb-carrying car got muddled about which street he was in, or found his time running out and abandoned the car in a panic—unknown to the man who was telephoning the warning.

Another problem for them is the car itself. This is usually hired or stolen. Hiring processes may give the police a clue. Theft may involve criminal gangs which are more likely than the terrorist gangs themselves to be penetrated by the police. An alternative—increasing ominously during 1974—was for the IRA to have the bomb placed by proxy, by kidnapping a father together with his wife or children, putting the bomb in his car, and forcing him to drive it to its target area, with the added warning that if he failed to get it there his wife or children would be shot.

As with other forms of bomb, alertness by police and public can play a major part. On 8th March 1973, the Price sisters, leading a gang of eleven, parked four cars in London with bombs in the boots. They had brought the cars across in the ferry from

Ireland with the bombs ready loaded. The police were alerted and, long before any telephone warning, had spotted one of the cars parked outside Police H.Q. in Scotland Yard where a constable had noticed that it was a 1967 model with a 'G' registration issued in 1969. He then saw that the number plate was freshly screwed on and called the bomb squad who disarmed the bomb. Two others, however, did go off, killing one person and wounding 243. Ten of the eleven bombers were caught on board an aircraft about to leave London Airport just before the bombs exploded.

HOAXES AND FALSE ALARMS

There are many times more hoax calls and false alarms than there are real bombs: there were 40 hoaxes per week in Belfast in 1974. The false alarms are genuine mistakes by the public, who may have reason for suspecting a package or a parked car and very properly report it. Some of the hoax calls are purely mischievous. Others are calculatedly made by the terrorists in order to induce a 'Wolf-Wolf' attitude towards the real calls when they come, or simply to cause added disruption—a further contribution to the aim of 'making life for ordinary people unbearable'.

BOOBY-TRAPS

There is no limit to the number of ways of setting booby-traps, using any of the fuses described in the last chapter—release, pull, pressure, tilt, electrical, chemical, photo-electric or remote control. The initiating mechanism can be fitted to a door, window, lid, light switch, television set, car boot, or to any attractive souvenir or unusual object which the victim may pick up or move. Pressure switches can be placed under mats, loose floorboards or rubble; trip wires can be concealed amongst debris or in long grass; tilt fuses can be concealed in almost any box or vase or other household object or in a sack or packing case in a garage or warehouse; or the killer with radio control may be watching from a window.

The surprising thing is that booby-traps are not set more often —either in conventional wars or by terrorists. The reason is that they are delicate and sensitive and experience has taught that they more often kill the would-be killer than his victim.

LIVING IN A MINEFIELD

If the intended victim, or the public, are alive to the threat of bombs or booby-traps and take the threat seriously, they are more than half-way to coming out alive.

All that the ordinary person can do, without technical training, is to have an idea of the kind of signs that are suspicious—about letters, parcels, shopping bags, suitcases, parked cars or potential booby-traps. Once suspicious he should isolate the object and call for the police bomb squad. He should not try to move it. He should not put it in water since water closes an electrical circuit. He should neither pull wires, nor cut them, as this may also set off the fuse. Tampering is foolhardy. It is extremely rare for anyone, once he has become suspicious of a bomb, to be blown up by it, if he has stuck to these rules.

IV. HIJACKING

Chapter Nine

The Politics of Air Piracy

THE GROWTH AND DECLINE OF HIJACKING

THERE have been about 450 recorded aircraft hijackings. Most of the early ones were regarded in the West with some sympathy: of the 21 hijackings in the seven years (1945–52) after World War II all but three were carried out by East European refugees escaping from Communist satellites.

It was not until 1958–59 that hijacking began to be used as an organized political weapon by Fidel Castro's brother Raúl in Cuba. This was followed by a brief see-saw by refugees of hijackings from Cuba to America and of American aircraft to Cuba. But this quickly blew over and the average number of hijackings from 1962–67 was only four per year. It was in 1968 that it suddenly, and explosively, became a world epidemic.

In that year there were 38 hijacking attempts. Of these, 32 were to Cuba and 23 were on flights originating in the U.S.A. Of the 38, 33 were successful—that is 87 per cent.

The peak year was 1969, with 82 hijack attempts, of which no less than 63 were to Cuba and 37 originated in the U.S.A. Since then, however, the number of attempts and the success rate have declined.[1]

CASTRO'S QUID PRO QUO

Just as 18 of the 21 hijackings from 1945–52 were by refugees escaping from Stalin's Eastern Europe, so 12 of the 18 between January 1959 and July 1961 were by refugees escaping from Castro's Cuba. They were received with acclamation in the

1. See page 119.

95

U.S.A., and whether or not they had killed anyone in the process there was no question of them being charged or handed back to Castro. Nor generally were the aircraft returned to Cuba. This, oddly enough, was on legal and commercial, rather than political grounds. A number of American firms had sued the Cuban Government in U.S. courts for seizure of assets or breaches of contract. Heavy damages were awarded and in default of payment the firms were entitled under U.S. law to claim property of the Cuban Government in the U.S.A. up to the value of the unpaid damages, by means of a writ of attachment. By July 1961 one particular firm (Harris Advertising Company of Miami) had seized nine of the planes hijacked from Cuba.[2]

Most of these planes were either elderly DC3s or light aircraft, worth only a few hundred thousand dollars in all. On 24th July, a naturalized American of Cuban origin, Wilfreda Oquendo, hijacked an Eastern Airlines Electra to Cuba. This was worth $3·3 million, and Castro—who returned the passengers and crew the next day—announced that he would not return the Electra until the Cuban planes seized under court orders were returned from the U.S.A. The Electra was eventually returned in exchange for a Cuban patrol boat which had been hijacked by another party of Cubans seeking asylum in the U.S.A.

This incident led to a rapid decline in hijacking, from both directions, between Cuba and the U.S.A. Castro, in fact, was a great deal harsher than most in dealing with hijackers. The hijacker of the Electra was imprisoned, and the only subsequent hijacker of a U.S. airliner to Cuba in 1961 was extradited to the point where the hijack had originated (in this case Mexico City), where he was tried and sentenced to eight years in jail. The planes, passengers and crew were returned to the U.S.A. without delay.

Cuba, of course, was under immediate threat of extinction if the United States chose to regard any such incident as an act of war and this must have influenced Castro's actions—for the Bay of Pigs invasion had taken place only three months earlier. It also no doubt influenced the decision of the Soviet Government to install the missiles which led to the Soviet-American Confrontation in October 1962.

2. David Phillips, *Skyjack* (London, Harrap, 1973, p. 48).

?ALESTINIANS GET THE IDEA

s time, however, the focus on hijacking had long since
from the Caribbean to the Middle East, and its chief
:nts have been the marxist Popular Front for the Liberation
:stine (PFLP). PFLP hijackings began in 1968, after the
lefeat in the 1967 war, which deprived them of nearly all
ind bases for *fedayeen* raids across Israel's borders. For
t year their attacks were all against El Al aircraft and were
d at airports in Europe. One aim was no doubt to frighten
;ers away from El Al and to deter European airport
ties from accepting them. Another aim frequently reiter-
PFLP's leader, Dr. Habbash, was to attract maximum
:y to their cause, which they certainly did—though Dr.
h's claim that they drew more publicity by attacking in
than in Israel had a taste of sour grapes about it. The
ate aim from the start, however, was the same as that of
tical kidnappers in Latin America, to exert blackmail for
ise of captured or convicted terrorists. Initially they had
ccess—even with the Israelis.
first Palestinian hijacking was on 23rd July 1968—
/ encouraged by five hijacks or attempted hijacks in the
:arlier in the same month. Three PFLP terrorists boarded
l 707 in Rome, bound for Tel Aviv, and diverted it to
where Tshombe was still held after his air kidnap). The
s released all the non-Israeli passengers and later
li women and children, holding only the plane and the
ale Israeli passengers and crew. They demanded the re-
,200 Arab guerrillas held in Israel, on the basis that the
ad said that the life of one Israeli was worth 100 Arabs.
:rnational Federation of Air Line Pilots Associations
:d that it would boycott all flights to Algeria, and the
onal Air Transport Federation said that it would call
mbers to refuse to service Algerian airliners unless the
d hostages were immediately released. After secret
ns through the Italian Consulate in Algiers, the
Government released the plane and the twelve hostages

There followed a lull of six years. '
hijackings in 1962, one in 1963, and thr
next three years. Amongst the seven in 19(
tic 'air kidnap' of Moise Tshombe, the (
who was under sentence of death. He
business trip into a private charter plane
criminal record, who then ordered the
Algiers. His aim was probably to seek s
the Algerian Government detained bot
victim until Tshombe died in prison tv

Suddenly, in 1968–70, there were 12
Cuba, over half of them from the U.S.A
seeking and there seems little doubt that
ment to him. A large number of these hi
after ransom money and they were g
victed or handed back for trial; others
some claimed to be political refugees a
of them were allowed to stay in Cuba,
elsewhere, and others were handed b
appeal as an automatic haven for the

Castro at times took pleasure in
Numerous loads of passengers and
comfort and hospitality with which t
awaiting return flights. He came do
landing of the first hijacked Jumbo i
amiable inspection of the aircraft w
go into the cabin 'as this might sc
airport authorities co-operated to the
putting down foam to receive one a
shot out, and providing every facili

Finally, the Cuban Government
in February 1973 by signing a fi
United States, covering both aircr
Government undertook either to r
prosecute them in their own courts
them severely. Since then, up to tl
later), there have been no hijacking
vice versa.

THE

By th
passec
expon
of Pal
Arab
their l
the firs
initiate
passeng
authori
ated b
publici
Habbas
Europe
immedi
the poli
the rele
some su
The
probabl
U.S.A.
an El A
Algiers (
Algerian
the Isra
twelve n
lease of
Israelis
The Int
announc
Internati
on its me
plane an
negotiatic
Algerian

when the Israelis agreed to release 16 Arab infiltrators caught during the Six Day War.

The PFLP then switched their efforts to attacking El Al aircraft on the ground in European airports—one at Athens on 26th December 1968 and another at Zurich on 18th February 1969, killing one Israeli in each case and wounding a number of others. Two PFLP terrorists were captured at Athens and three more at Zurich, a fourth being killed by an Israeli security guard who jumped from the aircraft and pursued them.

The Israelis had by now improved their security precautions on El Al aircraft, installing locked bullet-proofed cockpit doors and armed skymarshals. PFLP therefore switched their attacks to other aircraft and on 29th August 1969 Leila Khaled, who was to attract more publicity in later incidents, led a PFLP team which hijacked a TWA 707 (bound from Rome to Tel Aviv) to Damascus. After disembarkation of the passengers, they attempted to blow up the plane, though in the event it proved easily repairable. PFLP appeared to have no intention of kidnapping any of the passengers, but the Syrians decided to make use of them. Of the 101 on board, six were Israelis, though only two of these were males. The Syrians released all but these two, whom they eventually handed over, with the repaired plane, three months later, in exchange for thirteen Syrians held by Israel.

By December 1969, five more PFLP terrorists had been arrested in Athens—two in a raid on the El Al offices in the city in which they killed a two-year-old baby, and three who were caught attempting to board a TWA 707 at Athens airport, carrying guns and explosives in their hand baggage. They were discovered because an airport clerk became suspicious when he saw that all three carried identical bags. This brought the number of PFLP terrorists in custody in Greece to seven, with three more held in Switzerland.

On 22nd July 1970, two days before the trial in Athens of the two terrorists who had killed the baby in the El Al offices, six PFLP guerrillas hijacked an Olympic Airways 727 en route from Beirut to Athens. They directed it to land and then held its 55 passengers and crew as hostages in the plane, threatening to blow it up unless the seven prisoners were released. Through the mediation of the Red Cross it was agreed that the two killers would be tried, but then released regardless of their sentence, and that the other five would be released at the same time.

This left, in August 1970, three PFLP prisoners in Switzerland and three more, who had been captured in the meantime in an abortive attempt to seize an El Al 707 at Munich, in West Germany. It was with the aim of freeing these six, and at the same time attempting to show their domination over King Hussein of Jordan, that the PFLP launched the most complex multiple hijacking there had yet been. As their destination they selected an airstrip in Jordan itself. King Hussein had just agreed, with President Nasser of Egypt, on a cease-fire with Israel and this meant, in effect, that he had undertaken to control the Palestinian guerrillas operating against Israel from Jordan. Since one of the guerrillas' intermediate aims was to supplant Hussein's Bedouin régime in Amman with a Palestinian one, this did not suit the PFLP at all. So they intended to demonstrate that King Hussein could not control them even if he wanted to.

DAWSON'S FIELD

Dawson's Field was a natural dirt runway, marked out in the desert at the end of World War II by the R.A.F., forty miles north of Amman.

On Sunday 6th September 1970 two planes were hijacked and successfully diverted to Dawson's Field—a TWA 707 and a Swissair DC8. A third hijack had the same destination but went wrong: Leila Khaled and Patrick Arguello—a Latin American who had volunteered to serve with the PFLP—attempted to take over an El Al 707 bound for Tel Aviv which they had boarded at Amsterdam. They were overpowered by Israeli armed sky-marshals. Arguello was mortally wounded but Khaled was captured. The plane made a forced landing in London, where Khaled was handed over to the British police and held at Ealing Police Station.

Meanwhile there had been a fourth, unscheduled, hijack. Two PFLP terrorists who had been intended to board the plane with Leila Khaled were refused first class seats by El Al because they looked suspicious. Instead they boarded a TWA

Jumbo also flying from Amsterdam, hijacked it to Cairo (being uncertain whether it could land on Dawson's Field) and there blew it up—at a cost to the insurers of $20 million.

Two days later the PFLP, wanting a card to play for Leila Khaled, hijacked a British VC10 bound for London from Bahrain. Amongst its passengers this aircraft contained 21 unaccompanied British schoolchildren returning to school in England after holidays with parents serving overseas.

Five governments were now directly involved over the three aircraft on Dawson's Field: the Americans, the British and the Swiss, who owned the aircraft, and had many nationals as passengers—the two latter also holding PFLP prisoners. Also involved were the Germans, who held three more prisoners and had a number of passengers on the Swissair flight; and the Israelis, who also had passengers on Dawson's Field and, of course, held a very large number of Palestinian prisoners.

The attitudes of these Governments varied. The Israelis had moved from their earlier flexibility to an adamant refusal to give way to blackmail, whatever the cost. At the other end of the scale, the Germans and Swiss wanted to negotiate immediately and independently—no doubt with a view to giving way. The British prime minister took a middle line, agreeing that Leila Khaled and the other six terrorists in Germany and Switzerland should be released but only after *all* the hostages were freed, and he insisted that this would only be achieved if the five governments negotiated as a united front. This they did.

Meanwhile, King Hussein's army was besieging the airfield but they held back while various groups of passengers were released on various days—starting with 127 women and children, then 21 Arabs on the British plane when it arrived, and so on until eventually only 56 out of over 400 originally kidnapped remained in PFLP hands. They were removed to various refugee camps under PFLP control and the three planes were then blown up— at an insurance cost of $35 million borne by Lloyds of London. The 56 remaining hostages were either released or rescued by Hussein's army. When all were safely back, the British, Germans and Swiss, as promised, returned the seven prisoners to Cairo. This was on 10th October—five weeks after the original hijack.

HUSSEIN'S REACTION AND ARAB DISILLUSION WITH
HIJACKING

By that time King Hussein had turned his army, in force, upon
the guerrillas, and had virtually destroyed those who were in
Jordan; the remnants joining those already in Syria and the
Lebanon. After an initial Syrian army foray, on behalf of the
guerrillas, had been driven back, no one, Arab or otherwise,
raised a hand to help them. It was in mourning and revenge for
this disaster that the Black September Organization was formed
as a violent and militant wing of El Fatah—the 'moderate'
guerrillas who had been the main sufferers from Hussein's
reaction to the PFLP operation on Dawson's Field.

For the next year—until early 1972—Palestinian hijacks were
largely aimed at Jordanian planes, with very little success. Then,
on 22nd February 1972, Palestinian guerrillas, believed to be
from PFLP, but disclaimed by them, hijacked a Lufthansa Jumbo
to Aden. They released the passengers, but threatened to blow
up the Jumbo unless the airline paid a ransom of $5 million. They
did—the highest ransom ever paid up until that time.

Thereafter, hijacking became more intermingled with kidnapping and other forms of terrorist violence. After an attempted
hijacking on the ground on 9th May 1972 at Lod Airport (Tel
Aviv) had been thwarted by a bold Israeli attack, a mass, indiscriminate murder of passengers was carried out on 31st May at
the same airport by three Japanese acting on behalf of PFLP.
These two incidents are of interest mainly because of the facts
they reveal about the psychology and techniques of terrorists in
the air piracy field and they will therefore be described in the
next chapter.

There was, however, another significant hijacking after the
kidnapping and murder of eleven Israeli athletes by Black
September terrorists at the Munich Olympics in September
1972. Five of the eight terrorists were killed and three captured
alive and held in West Germany.

To secure the release of these three, two Black September
terrorists hijacked a Lufthansa 727 to Zagreb, ordering it to

refuel there, go to Munich, collect the three captured terrorists and take them to Libya. The Germans agreed at once, though, for a variety of reasons, arising from bad weather, fuel problems and the terrorists' suspicion of German delay in actually producing the prisoners, the aircraft returned to Zagreb and the prisoners joined it there instead, to fly to Tripoli.

As soon as the three had originally been captured in Munich, it was clear to everyone that the Palestinians would hijack a German aircraft to secure their release and that the Germans— in the run-up to a general election—would give way. One writer has gone so far as to suggest that the actual hijacking was a ritual performance, secretly agreed by both sides, so as to go through the process with the minimum of damage.[3]

There was, however, a growing Arab disillusion with hijacking. In December 1973 eight Palestinian terrorists murdered 33 people in aircraft on the ground in Rome and Athens. They then hijacked the aircraft and took off on what proved to be a tour of Arab countries, every one of which, including Libya, refused them permission to land and physically blocked the runways to prevent them from doing so.

Then in February 1974 a mixed group of Palestinians and Japanese hijacked a ferry after an abortive attempt to blow up an oil refinery on an island off Singapore. The Singapore police held the ferry under armed surveillance. At this the PFLP switched their pressure far across the world, occupying the Japanese Embassy in Kuwait, and holding members of the staff as hostages. The Japanese agreed to provide an aircraft to pick up the terrorists in Singapore and fly them to Kuwait, where the Government initially refused them permission to land, but gave way in the face of a threat to kill the Embassy staff.

The reason for the growing reluctance of Arab Governments to co-operate with Palestinian terrorists is probably due to their double success in October 1973. Firstly in wiping out the humiliation of the 1948, 1956 and 1967 Arab-Israeli wars and secondly, in proving that the oil weapon was far more effective than terrorism, in exerting influence on the United States and

3. Peter Clyne, *An Anatomy of Skyjacking* (London, Abelard-Schuman, 1973, p. 150).

West European powers and in persuading them in turn to exert pressure on Israel.

At the same time hijacking was losing favour elsewhere in the world, and especially in the United States, due to the success of security measures. Before considering these, however, it is worth looking in more detail at some examples of what the terrorists actually do, in aircraft and in airports, in the conduct of air piracy.

Chapter Ten

Hijackers - Their Character and Techniques

WHO, HOW AND WHY

THE motivation of the Palestinian hijackers has been wholly political. Their aims have been the release of prisoners, ransom for their funds, political coercion of governments and—perhaps above all—publicity for their cause. The majority of other hijackers, however, have not acted for political dividends. Many —like the post-war Czechs and Rumanians and the Cubans fleeing from Castro—have done it as refugees or as men on the run, seeking a means of transport to asylum or sanctuary. Still more hijacks have been done by crackpots or by criminals for monetary gain.

The technical process of hijacking is very simple. Two weapons predominate: the pistol, easily concealed in pockets, hand baggage or even in a wig; and the hand grenade which, when held in the hijacker's hand with the pin out, is a decisive deterrent against anyone trying to shoot or overpower him, since if he relaxes his grip on the release lever everyone dies.

Jet aircraft are extremely vulnerable and with up to 400 people aboard a Jumbo, valued at $20 million, the blackmail stakes are high. Contrary to popular misconception, however, they are not vulnerable to the puncturing of a pressurized fuselage. The risk of 'explosive decompression' is a myth, because the cabin compressors pump in air at a much faster rate than it can escape through a bullet hole.[1] The risks are of fire, of damage to the controls, and of incapacitation of the pilot.

1. James Pyle, of the U.S. Federal Aviation Administration, speaking in 1961. Cited in Phillips, *op. cit.* (p. 230).

105

Though there is little mystery about the weapons, however, there is much to be learned about the way in which terrorists behave and react to various events. The following examples are chosen from political and criminal hijackings, some in the air and some on the ground.

LEILA KHALED

Leila Khaled was born in Haifa in 1944 and her family became refugees in Lebanon in 1948, when she was four years old. When she was a student she became a marxist and joined the PFLP, dedicated to the belief that the Israelis could only be driven out of Palestine by force. Since Palestine, to her, meant the whole of Israel, including the coastal plain, this was undoubtedly true. Like most other Palestinians, however, she exercised her use of force outside Israel and mainly outside the Middle East. The first plane for whose hijacking she was responsible was not an Israeli plane and only six of its 101 passengers were Israelis.

Khaled, assisted by a male terrorist, Salim Essawi, boarded a TWA 707 in Rome and hijacked it to Damascus. On the way, however, she ordered it to circle Lod Airport at Tel Aviv (its original destination) to cock a snook at the Israelis, and then ordered it to fly over her birthplace, Haifa.

She had a strong sense of 'public relations' and was the prototype of the swashbuckling girl guerrilla with a gun at her hip—the female equivalent of Fidel Castro in the Sierra Maestra. Patricia Hearst and others have since tried to copy her. While in the air, with the passengers at her mercy, Khaled announced that none, not even the Israelis, would be held as hostages, but would be free to go wherever they chose as soon as the plane landed. She thanked them for their co-operation—and wished them a happy journey.[2]

Her second hijack attempt, against the El Al 707 flying from Amsterdam on 6th September 1970, was defeated by the Israeli skymarshals on board. She and her assistant, Patrick Arguello,

2. Phillips, *op. cit.* (p. 135). In the event, however, as recorded in the previous chapter, the Syrian Government retained two of the Israelis to drive their own political bargain.

both carried grenades. Arguello had pulled the pin out of his grenade and he released the lever when he was shot by the sky-marshals. Luckily it had a weak spring and failed to fire. Leila Khaled had not, however, pulled the pin out of her grenade and she was overpowered without injury to either side. Her failure to press home her attack—in contrast to Arguello—was to influence the Israelis in dealing with a later hijacking involving women guerrillas at Lod Airport, which is described further on in this chapter.

HIJACKING FOR MONEY

On 10th November 1972 three black Americans, two of them on bail accused of rape, and the third an escaped convict, hijacked a Southern Airways DC9 flying from Birmingham, Alabama.

The hijack began soon after take-off. The leader of the team, Henry Jackson, who was sitting four seats from the front, called an air hostess on the pretence that someone was sick, grabbed her round the neck, pulled her to the cockpit door, kicked it open and pointed a pistol at the pilot. His two accomplices, also with pistols, simultaneously rose from their seats at the back of the plane. One, Lewis Moore, was a close associate of Jackson and the other, Melvin Cale, was Moore's half-brother.

Afraid that the male passengers might be concealing weapons, the hijackers ordered all to strip down to their underwear. Their clothes—with the women's handbags—were collected and the stewardesses were required to search them before returning them two hours later.

Jackson and Moore had a grievance against the mayor and police of the city of Detroit, whom they had unsuccessfully sued for $4 million for brutality when they had been arrested on a charge of concealing weapons 18 months earlier. After the plane had made a short refuelling stop at Jackson, Mississippi, they directed it to Detroit, where they circled the airport and demanded by radio a ransom of $10 million, in default of which, they said they would crash the plane on the atomic plant at Oak Ridge, Tennessee.

It was after 10 p.m., and the mayor of Detroit said that as all the banks were closed he had no way of raising the money before the next morning. By this time the weather was too bad to land at Detroit so the hijackers agreed that the plane should instead land to refuel at Cleveland, Ohio, where they ordered it to park on the floodlit apron close to the terminal building. They demanded that the refuelling should be done by one man, stripped to his underpants. All of the maintenance men refused to do this, so it was done by an FBI agent. Meanwhile a raiding party of FBI and police tried to stalk the plane from the rear, where they hoped they could not be seen, but the plane taxied away to take off before they could reach it.

The hijackers then directed the plane to Toronto and warned that if the $10 million was not waiting there, they would make for Oak Ridge and crash the plane there as threatened. Southern Airways had meanwhile sent another aircraft to Toronto with $500,000 and this landed at 4.30 a.m., just before the hijacked aircraft. The hijackers refused to settle for this and at 6.15 a.m. the plane, after refuelling, took off again for Oak Ridge—or rather the nearby airport at Knoxville—which they circled for five hours, before again landing to refuel, and taking off again just before 10 a.m. They resumed circling over Knoxville and, after further negotiations by radio, they landed at 1.30 p.m. at Chattanooga, Tennessee, where they were refuelled by another man stripped down to his underpants. He also passed $2 million in bags through the cockpit window—half a million provided each by the airline and the City of Detroit, and a million by the Federal Government. The aircraft took off again at 2.30 p.m. and the stewardesses were ordered to check the money. The aircraft then landed at Havana, where Cale remained on board and held the aircraft under his gun while Jackson and Moore disembarked to check that the Cubans would receive them and allow them to keep the money. When they were refused Jackson and Moore returned furiously to the plane and they took off again. They told the pilot that they wanted to be flown with their money to Switzerland and, on his advice, the plane landed at Orlando, Florida, to collect navigation data and to refuel. By this time it was dark again—the second night had begun.

Just as refuelling was completed, FBI agents opened fire and punctured the tyres. Furiously the hijackers shot the co-pilot in the shoulder and threatened to shoot all the passengers, one by one, unless the aircraft took off—flat tyres or no. They made a nightmare take-off, with sparks flying, and the engines became overheated with pieces of rubber being inhaled into the jets. After circling President Nixon's home at Key Biscayne, they landed again at Havana just after midnight—after a 29 hour hijack. The exhausted hijackers were arrested and the money seized. The passengers and crew were flown to Miami next day— where they gave their pilot, Captain Haas, a standing ovation.[3]

This hijack was the final straw and brought the U.S. and Cuba together to sign their five-year agreement.[4]

A variant of the criminal hijack, fashionable in the U.S.A. in 1971–72, was the parachute hijack, in which the hijacker—realizing that he would have little chance of escaping with his ransom if he landed at an airport—tried to parachute into a remote area with his loot. Only one—the first—did get away with it and it is not known whether he is alive or dead as no trace of him, his parachute, or his money, was ever seen again. All the others were arrested in the air, on the ground, or were killed.

ATTACKING THE HIJACKERS ON THE GROUND

One of the earliest examples of a criminal hijacking had been frustrated by shooting at the tyres of the aircraft and this was no doubt in the minds of the FBI during the Jackson/Moore/Cale hijacking described above. The earlier hijacking was an attempt by an American convict on parole—Leon Bearden—to escape to Cuba on 3rd August 1961 with his 16-year-old son Cody. He had initially hijacked the aircraft—a Continental 707—on a flight from Phoenix, Arizona, and had put down to refuel at El Paso, Texas, where he released everyone except the crew and four passengers kept as hostages. These four, unknown to him, included a volunteer, who was a plain-clothes Border Patrolman, Leonard Gillman.

3. There is a detailed account of this hijacking, along with a number of other valuable case studies and statistics in David Phillips' *Skyjack*.
4. See page 97.

This hijack occurred in the middle of the highly-charged negotiations between the U.S. and Cuban Governments over Castro's retention of the Electra aircraft, kept as a retort to the U.S. seizure, under court orders, of nine Cuban planes hijacked by anti-Castro refugees, and described in the previous chapter. It was wrongly assumed that Bearden was a Cuban and this affected President Kennedy's handling of the case. It is certainly possible that Bearden may have planned to hand the 707 to Castro as an additional bargaining counter, in the hope of receiving a rich reward to live on in Cuba.

After refuelling, the plane began to taxi to the runway for take-off, but FBI agents drove alongside it and flattened the tyres with machine-gun fire from Border Patrol Cars. The hijacker shouted desperately at the pilot to keep going, but the plane ground to a halt, slumped on its damaged undercarriage. Bearden, now thoroughly dispirited, agreed to an FBI agent coming aboard to negotiate, and while they were talking, three of the four hostages crept out by the rear door and the fourth— Leonard Gillman, the plain-clothes Border Patrolman—seized a moment when Bearden's attention was distracted to hit him on the jaw. Though the blow broke Gillman's hand he was able to place an armlock on Bearden and the attempt was over.

Another hijack attempt was foiled on the ground at Lod Airport, Tel Aviv, on 9th May 1972, and this again underlined some of the weaknesses of hijackers on the ground. Four Palestinian terrorists—two men and two girls—had boarded a Sabena 707 in Brussels carrying a remarkable arsenal of arms and explosives. The two girls each carried a grenade in a box of cosmetics. They wore special girdles made of a high explosive fabric and they had electric detonators tucked into their brassières. The men carried revolvers and a battery to fire the detonators.

Soon after take-off, the girls went to the washrooms to remove their explosive girdles and then tucked them under their seats. The girls—Rima Tannous (21) and Theresa Halaseh (19)—had been made responsible for the firing of the explosives, if ordered to do so by the team leader.

The two men then produced their pistols, hijacked the aircraft and ordered it to proceed to its destination—Lod Airport, Tel Aviv, where they declared that the aircraft, with themselves, the crew and all the passengers (50 of whom were Israelis) would be blown up unless 100 Arab prisoners were released by the Israelis.

Defence minister Moshe Dayan arrived in the control tower to take personal charge of the negotiations. The plane had touched down at 7.15 p.m. and the British pilot, Captain Levy, parked it a mile from the terminal building. Under cover of darkness Dayan sent two airport workers to crawl under the aircraft, let down the tyres and drain off the hydraulic fluid from the undercarriage.

The hijackers were initially unaware that the aircraft had been immobilized and Dayan played for time until it was light. He had the plane refuelled and then (when the immobilization was discovered) discussed the possibility of making another plane available. By 10 a.m., however, the leader of the team, Rafat, lost patience and ordered the girls to blow up the plane. They began crying and kissing each other and one of them moved towards the explosives. Captain Levy, thinking that there was nothing more to lose, attacked Rafat and got hold of his revolver, but let go when the other male terrorist intervened with his gun. The diversion, however, had the effect of taking their minds off blowing up the aircraft.

At noon, Rafat allowed Levy, accompanied by a Red Cross negotiator, to talk to Dayan in the control tower. He tried to convince Dayan that the terrorists really did intend to blow up the plane. Dayan also took note from the discussion that the two male terrorists with guns remained at the front of the aircraft and that the two girls stayed with the explosives at the rear. This helped him to make his plan of attack. Among other things, remembering that Leila Khaled had failed to press home her attack in 1970, and with Levy's description of the girls' agitation when Rafat had earlier given them the order to fire, Dayan was confident that they would, in the event, shrink from blowing themselves up with the aircraft.

Levy was not given any indication that the plane was to be attacked, and he returned to it under the Red Cross flag.

At 3.45 p.m. 18 Israeli commandos in mechanics' overalls approached the aircraft with the apparent intention of repairing the undercarriage. The Red Cross man, who had secured an undertaking from both sides not to use force, was being taken aboard under his supervision, when he suspected that these 'mechanics' were not what they seemed. He talked to the terrorists, who allowed three of the crew off the plane to search them. They found nothing, but before the crew members had re-embarked the 'mechanics' had produced guns and the attack began. They had by that time split into three groups: beside the front and rear doors, and under the wings where the emergency doors were located. At a given signal they simultaneously leaped up ladders, shot the doors open and broke in, shouting at the passengers to stay seated. Only one passenger, who stood up, was killed. Both the male terrorists were shot dead. One of the girls was holding the battery and the detonator wire, ready to fire the explosives. The other held a grenade with the pin out. Both were very frightened and surrendered; the one with the grenade, turning her hand up, so that the Israeli commando could grasp the lever and take it without it blowing up.[5]

Stars in the Sky

Three weeks later—on 30th May 1972—the PFLP employed three Japanese terrorists to avenge the raid on the Sabena aircraft. Although not a hijacking, the operation was air piracy and had a big influence on the actions at that time being discussed for countering hijacking, and on the understanding of just how far a really fanatical terrorist might be prepared to go.

The three Japanese were members of the extreme marxist Red Army Fraction which had earlier broken away from the Japanese Communist Party. All were students or ex-students. After training in weapons and explosives in Japan and North Korea, they volunteered for service with the PFLP and were further trained, especially in the use of Czech Kalashnikov rifles, explosives and grenades, in a refugee camp in Lebanon.

On 16th May—a week after the Sabena incident—they began to train specifically for a revenge operation at Lod. On 22nd May they flew via Paris to Frankfurt where they were given forged

5. Phillips, *op. cit.* (p. 162), in which this operation is described in detail, with photographs.

passports. On 24th May they travelled by train from Frankfurt to Rome, where on 30th May they were provided with suitcases containing Kalashnikov rifles and grenades.

That afternoon they boarded an Air France plane bound for Tel Aviv. Their baggage was not searched. The rule at Rome airport was that the baggage of passengers joining foreign aircraft was searched only if the airline requested it. Air France made no such request in this case.

On arrival at Lod Airport, the three Japanese collected their baggage from the conveyors, removed the guns and opened fire, indiscriminately, on the people in the crowded baggage hall. Twenty-four people—mainly Puerto Rican Christian pilgrims on their way to Bethlehem and Jerusalem—were killed, and 72 were wounded. Two of the Japanese were killed, one by the crossfire and the other by his own hand; the third, Kozo Okamoto, was captured.

At his trial, Okamoto was sentenced to life imprisonment—and his release has since been one of the declared aims of a number of Palestinian hijackings in 1973 and 1974. He clearly wished, however, to die. He made a full confession only on the promise that he would be given a pistol and allowed to shoot himself, but the promise was not kept. His testimony contained some revealing statements:

'Revolutionary war is warfare for justice, which I define as creating a society with no class struggle. War involves killing and destruction. We cannot limit warfare to the destruction of buildings. We believe that the killing of human beings is inevitable . . . The incident has been reported worldwide, but, it seems to me nobody has grasped the motivation for it. But when a similar operation takes place the next time, what will the world think? . . . The Arab world lacks spiritual fervour, so we felt that through this attempt we could probably stir up the Arab World . . . We three soldiers, after we die, want to become three stars of Orion . . . I believe that some of those we slaughtered have become stars in the sky . . . The revolution will go on and there will be many more stars.'[6]

6. Quoted in Peter Clyne's *An Anatomy of Skyjacking*, which gives an excellent account of Okamoto's trial.

This incident shocked the world as no previous air piracy had done before, more so even than the later killing of 33 people at Athens and Rome Airports in December 1973. It brought home the full potential of human callousness and fanaticism. It indicated that the only counter to men prepared to go this far, was to prevent them or their baggage ever getting into the air-transport pipeline, at whatever cost; and it also revealed the extent of the Palestinians' international organization. Japanese terrorists, trained in Japan, North Korea and Lebanon, had been provided with false papers in Germany, and Czech weapons in Rome, to board a French aircraft in order to attack international air travellers in Israel. In at least five of these countries there must clearly have been underground cells to serve them, manned either by Arab refugees, immigrants or students in Europe or— as in the case of the Japanese—by sympathetic marxist movements operating in those countries. All of this was co-ordinated from a headquarters in the sanctuary of a refugee camp in Lebanon. Air piracy had become an international conspiracy to be answered only by international collaboration on behalf of the travelling public.

Chapter Eleven

Countering The Hijacker

THE MAN WITH LICE IN HIS BEARD

'IF we allow a little pipsqueak like Castro, with lice in his beard, to defy the United States of America, nobody is going to have any respect for us.' This was how a U.S. congressman summed up the mood of the House—still smarting under the humiliation of the Bay of Pigs fiasco—about the hijacking of three American aircraft to Cuba in 1961.

President Kennedy and Fidel Castro were both alive to the risk of war and both 'kept their cool'. Castro returned the planes and passengers and imprisoned or extradited the hijackers. Kennedy made hijacking a Federal Offence punishable by death (though no hijacker has in the event been executed in the U.S.A.) and installed armed skymarshals on selected flights.

One congressman proposed that all passengers should be obliged to pass through a gate containing metal detectors, but this was not in the event to be introduced until more than ten years later.

After a lull of six years came the violent mushrooming of hijackings in 1968–69. By the end of 1972, a total of 159 American aircraft had been hijacked, of which 85 were to Cuba. It was only then—at the beginning of 1973—that effective measures to counter hijacking were introduced into the U.S.A., and an effective agreement signed with Castro. Although this followed immediately upon the spectacular hijacking of the DC9 to Cuba by Jackson, Moore and Cale, described in the previous chapter, this was only the last straw and a more powerful motivation was in fact the series of far more bloody and destructive political hijackings by Palestinian terrorists.

SELECTIVE SEARCHING

During the hijacking boom of 1968–70, there were 14,000 domestic flights every day in the U.S.A. and another 300 overseas flights from U.S. airports. There were 150 million passengers carried each year and the problem of searching all of them seemed insoluble.

Magnetometers, capable of detecting metal of the density normally found in a gun or grenade, were by that time available. A model, suitable for an arch through which passengers would pass,was priced at $1,000 and hand searching models at $100.

A Task Force, set up in 1969 to deal with the problem, decided that 100 per cent search was neither feasible nor necessary. The great majority of air travellers were businessmen who travelled regularly, and these—and many others—could be quickly eliminated from those to be searched. Various forms of profile were attempted, not so much to detect suspicious persons as to eliminate unsuspicious ones. One of these profiles was to eliminate all except those between 16 and 65 who had bought a single ticket for cash. Surprisingly this left only 2 per cent to be searched. Other profiles—which were kept confidential—further narrowed this to half of 1 per cent.

These few selected for search were passed through the magnetometer. If it detected anything, they were interviewed and invited to submit to a full search. If they declined, they were politely informed that the airline could not carry them (there was a notice to this effect at the entrances to the terminal building).

The trials of these measures were given a big boost in October 1969 when Raffael Minchiniello, an ex-marine, boarded a TWA 707 with a fantastic armoury of grenades and automatic weapons, including a rifle in a fishing rod case, and diverted the aircraft nearly 7,000 miles to Italy.

In that month three airlines—Pan Am, TWA and Eastern— adopted the system. During the next six months, by May 1970, they had screened 226,000 passengers. Ninety-nine and a half per cent were cleared by the profile, leaving 1,268 to be searched by the magnetometer, which cleared another 630, leaving 638 to be interviewed. The interview cleared 334, and the other 304 agreed to be searched. Twenty-four were denied boarding, and most of these were arrested for carrying either hard drugs or weapons. The main effect was no doubt to deter potential hijackers and airport authorities reported finding a number of guns hastily stuffed into pot plants in the assembly lounges. From the time they began to use the system, Eastern Airlines had only two hijackings in the subsequent 11 months, compared with 16 in the previous 13 months.[1] Overall, however, hijackings were continuing at a high rate, the majority by fugitives and criminals.

A HUNDRED PER CENT SEARCH AT THE BOARDING GATES

It was, eventually, the most spectacular of all political hijackings—which took place at Dawson's Field in September 1970—that put in motion the process which was to reduce hijacking in the U.S.A. to negligible proportions by 1973. The President appointed a retired U.S. army Lieutenant General, Benjamin O. Davis, as Director of Aviation Security, to co-ordinate the whole anti-hijack programme. Davis was a remarkable man on any count. His father had been the first black cadet at West Point and the first to reach the rank of Major General. Benjamin junior broke that record.

He realized that skymarshals and locked flight deck doors could only be a deterrent. Experience up to 1970 had shown that the majority of hijackings, once initiated, were successful in getting the aircraft to where the hijackers wanted it. The aircraft and its passengers had proved too vulnerable for effective resistance in the air.

Nor would the prospect of capture or death be enough to deter them. A fanatic like Okamoto would no more be deterred by logical reasoning than would a wild animal. The only answer was a barrier through which he or his weapons could not pass.

So Davis was convinced that the problem had to be tackled on the ground—at the boarding gates. He set himself the target of

1. Phillips, *op. cit.* (p. 239).

making it mandatory for 100 per cent of passengers, before embarking on any commercial airliner in the U.S.A., to submit to a search of themselves, their hand baggage and their hold baggage. It was in 1972, the year of Okamoto, which Davis described as the pivotal year, that he decided that this scheme could, and must, be implemented.

The equipment—the magnetometer arches and the magnetic and electronic hand searchers—were now available in adequate numbers. Davis realized, however, that this was a secondary part of the problem. Equipment was useless unless it was conscientiously used on every passenger and his baggage. Otherwise the two or three who mattered, out of the hundreds of thousands entering a big airport, would be the ones who would get through. And this depended on the *total* co-operation of the airlines and airport authorities, and on the willing acceptance of these measures by the travelling public.

The solution lay in deploying enough searchers and enough equipment at every U.S. airport to ensure that the passengers and their baggage could be searched *faster* than they could check in after the search at the ticket counter in the boarding lobby. The queue must be at the boarding lobby entrance, not at the search barrier. Otherwise, after any kind of delay or any build-up of a passenger back-log, some official, harassed by impatient managements fearful of losing traffic, was bound to say 'Oh hell, we're half-an-hour late already—let 'em through.' But as long as it was never the search that was the bottle-neck, this would not happen.

On 5th January 1973 this process became mandatory throughout the U.S.A. In the next two years (to January 1975) there were only three hijack attempts in aircraft originating their flights in the U.S.A.—and all three failed.

The full figures for 1968–73 underline Davis's achievement.[2]

Screening and searching were done entirely by the airline personnel in the presence of armed guards provided by the airport authorities. The cost was borne by the airlines and air-

2. Worldwide figures up to 1972 taken from *Strategic Survey* 1972 published by the International Institute for Strategic Studies in London. Figures for the U.S.A. and for 1973 compiled from U.S. State Department figures and press reports.

	WORLDWIDE			ORIGINATING IN U.S.A.		
YEAR	TOTAL ATTEMPTS	HIJACK SUCCEEDED	PER CENT SUCCESS	TOTAL ATTEMPTS	HIJACK SUCCEEDED	PER CENT SUCCESS
1968	38	33	87	23	20	87
1969	82	70	85	37	31	82
1970	72	46	64	14	11	77
1971	61	24	39	29	13	44
1972	64	18	28	29	12	41
1973	22	11	50	3	nil	nil

ports—and, thus, indirectly by the passengers in the price of their tickets.

During 1973, 3,500 intending passengers were prevented from passing the boarding gates at the 531 airports in the U.S.A. Of these, 300 declined to be searched and so were turned away. The other 3,200 were arrested. From them were seized 2,000 guns, 3,500 lb. of high explosives and 23,000 knives and other lethal weapons.[3] Many of the weapons, admittedly, were carried by girls for self-protection in a violent land, but they had seen the warning and ignored it. The result was a dramatic decline in hijacking, and a huge dose of encouragement to the people fighting the war against all kinds of terrorism world-wide. It showed that 'impossible' problems could be overcome.

THE FUTURE

Air piracy will never be wholly banished from the world, though, like sea piracy two centuries ago, it can be reduced to tolerable proportions by collaboration between the nations concerned.

As encouraging as the success at the boarding gates in the U.S.A., has been the growing collaboration between the nations of the world. Following the Dawson's Field hijacking, delegates of 76 nations attended a Convention for the Suppression of Unlawful Seizure of Aircraft. The Convention was adopted by 74 votes to nil with two (Algeria and Chile) abstaining, and was

3. Figures provided by U.S. State Department.

signed immediately by 50 of them. There were some important absentees, including Cuba and a number of Arab countries—though Cuba has shown willingness to sign bilateral treaties instead.

The Arab countries—as described earlier—are also discreetly co-operating, and Palestinian hijackers are now finding most Arab runways blocked against them.

It remains to be seen whether the decline is a permanent one or whether, as after the lull of 1962–66, the disease will break out again. If it does, then the world may be driven to more drastic measures to compel states which give sanctuary to hijackers to hand them over, either to the country to whom the aircraft belonged, or to the country in which the hijacker boarded it, or possibly to some international agency.

A comprehensive plan for an international 'Air Crimes Commission' (ACC) has been proposed by Peter Clyne.[4] This Commission would run its own International Court and its own International Prison. Member countries in which hijackers landed would undertake to arrest them and hand them over for trial by this court, regardless of their country of origin. If found guilty, they would be imprisoned beyond the control of any member state. If any member state failed to comply, all other members would be obliged to boycott it, by denying landing facilities to any of its aircraft and by refusing to fly their own aircraft to its airports. The same boycott would apply to any country which declined to join the Commission or to enforce its rules.

This is an idealistic solution. There is at present no prospect of the countries which are likely to be the main offenders committing themselves to such a blanket undertaking. Arab countries, in particular, for the time being, still have the same underlying sympathy for Palestinian hijackers as the Western countries had for East European refugees in 1947–52 and the U.S. had for Cuban refugees in 1959–61. If, however, there were another serious epidemic of hijacking, the exasperation these countries have already begun to show, might drive them to do something along the lines Peter Clyne has proposed.

4. *op. cit.* (p. 166).

V. TACKLING THE DISEASE

Chapter Twelve

The Character and Motivation of the Terrorist

GOOD GUYS AND BAD GUYS

WE have thus far been concerned mainly with the techniques of the terrorist and with how these can best be countered. Anyone who has to live with terrorism, to protect himself against it or to defeat it, also needs to understand the character and motivation of the terrorist. Although, as has been pointed out, the way to defeat the terrorist is to keep him out, like a poisonous snake, it can be argued that even poisonous snakes have their place in the balance of nature. Moreover, the terrorist is more intelligent and resourceful than a snake and has political and intellectual, as well as merely instinctive motives. It is as great a mistake to underestimate his dedication as it is to underestimate his difficulties.

It is also a mistake to underestimate the degree to which the guerrilla can attract public support—particularly if this is based on an appeal to nationalism rather than to a political theory, such as marxism or anarchism. This differentiates, for example, the Palestinian guerrillas and the IRA from movements like the Tupamaros or the ERP. Whether guerrillas are seen as 'good guys' or 'bad guys' depends largely on the eye of the beholder.

The Spanish *guerrilleros* fighting to drive Napoleon out of Spain in 1808 were seen by most of their fellow countrymen and by the British as 'good guys'. So were the resistance fighters or partisans trying to drive the Germans out of France and Russia in 1944. They regarded it as their right and duty to kill; unable to fight as uniformed soldiers, they killed by stealth; bitterly resentful of the invading soldiers they were brutally cruel to any whom they caught. The occupying armies, already overstretched, regarded the partisans as more deserving of death than the uniformed enemy soldiers, and to deter them they answered cruelty with cruelty. In their attempts to deter the local population from supporting the partisans they slid down a slippery slope. From seeking friendly co-operation, to applying strict population control and from thence to torture, reprisals and the seizing of hostages was a fatal progression. Death—on both sides—was commonplace. How far the activities of the guerrillas advanced their cause militarily is arguable, but they certainly provided a focus for what survived of national morale.

A number of the partisans' fellow countrymen resented their activities because they themselves were reluctant to risk their livelihood, or still worse the arrest of the family bread-winner, lest they be unable to provide for their children. Fearful of reprisals, they declined to support the resistance—and were sometimes punished at the time or after the war as 'collaborators'. The proportion of Frenchmen, and of Ukranians and other Soviet citizens who collaborated with the Germans, at least passively, was much larger than many people now find it convenient to remember. Nevertheless—certainly by the end of the war—the majority of the people were behind the partisans and regarded them as heroes.

It is not always easy, in those circumstances, to be sure who does, in his heart, support guerrilla violence, or to know how far he is prepared to go in his support. Probably the majority of people try to keep out of it either way, and bend with the wind as far as they have to. Nevertheless, in the face of a foreign army occupying their country by conquest, the underlying sympathy will nearly always be with the guerrillas—with 'our own boys'.

How far does this apply to the Palestinians? To the Northern Irish? To the people in Latin American dictatorships? To the American public or the British public in relation to groups using political violence in their countries?

And how far, in each case, do the guerrillas themselves perceive their public support? How far do they think this support to be relevant or necessary to justify their violence? Whether justified or not, terrorism can best be regarded as a drastic and dangerous drug. It may be that it is, in the end, better to suffer from the effects of this drug for a time in order to overcome a worse disease—such as occupation by an unwanted foreign army, oppression by an unwanted dictator, or gross oppression of a defenceless minority—just as it may be necessary to accept the effects of a powerful drug in order to drive out a malignant growth or to accept amputation in order to kill a potentially lethal infection. Sometimes the drug—like terrorism—however justified its use may have seemed, leaves the patient with a worse disease than it aimed to cure. Terrorism most often does no good and much harm.

THE PALESTINIANS

The Palestinian guerrillas are the most publicised of the groups currently using terror as a weapon, though both the ERP and the IRA may have killed more people in the 1970s so far, and there may be other groups in remote parts of Africa and Asia killing more still, without hitting any headlines. The Palestinians have also had a claim to a loyal base, even though it is fragmented and outside Palestine itself—in the refugee camps. They have also enjoyed the sympathy and financial support of the rich Arab world, though there are signs that this support is waning.

It is fruitless to argue about who has the right to own Palestine. It has been conquered repeatedly by different peoples: by the children of Israel 3,500 years ago; by the Romans 2,000 years ago; by the Arabs 1,300 years ago; and by the Ottoman Turks 500 years ago. They, in turn, were driven out by the Allied Armies in 1918 after ambiguous and conflicting promises, on the one hand to restore Arab rule, and on the other hand to found in Palestine a National Home for the Jews.

For over a thousand years Jew and Arabs have both owned property there, side by side. By 1947, virtually all the fertile land which had been owned by Arabs on the coastal plain had been bought by individual Jews or by the National Land Fund of the Jewish Agency located in Jerusalem. It was this land—almost precisely—which was allocated, by a large majority vote in the United Nations, to the Jews in the Partition Plan implemented in 1948.

Thereafter the Arabs made several attempts to regain this land by force. In 1948-49 they gained none and lost more; in 1967 more still. In 1973, though they regained a little of the Sinai desert, they regained none of Palestine.

The essential political factor in the motivation of the Palestinian terrorist groups is that Palestine to them means *all* of Palestine, including every inch of the fertile plain which was the original territory allocated to Israel by the United Nations in 1948. The United Nations has frequently voted in favour of the restoration of the land seized by the Israeli army after 1949, but never in favour of the restoration of the land allocated in 1948—in other words for the extinction of the State of Israel. The Palestinian guerrillas are therefore fighting the world—and they themselves feel that they are fighting the world; and since they have lost not only the fertile land, but also every inch of territory that ever bore the name of Palestine, they feel that they have nothing to lose. This accounts for their desperation.

For the overwhelming majority of Palestinian refugees, their desperation is that of defeat and of a listless life, without hope, in a refugee camp. A very small proportion (about 1 per cent) join the various armed groups. Most of these have thus far undergone training only (mainly in Syria). The even smaller proportion (about 0·2 per cent) who have fought in the active guerrilla groups are largely found from, and led by, those with higher than average education. Many have been outside the refugee camps for education and for work, and could, if they wished, earn a prosperous living elsewhere in the Middle East (as do many educated Palestinians in Kuwait and other countries), or as immigrants to Europe. Many of them have, in fact, taken jobs or entered universities in Europe, under cover of which they conduct their terrorist operations. Others have returned to full-time service in guerrilla units based in refugee camps in Syria and Lebanon.

Superimposed on their nationalistic motivation, some of the Palestinian guerrilla groups have also a political motivation as marxists, and this gives them something in common with the other intellectual terrorist groups in Latin America, North America and Europe.

If, as seems inevitable, the rest of the Arab world settles for a political solution which recognizes the permanence of an Israel with frontiers approximating to those of 1948–49, then the Palestinian terrorists may well concentrate their attack on countries such as Egypt, Syria and Saudi Arabia. If so, they may find themselves as tragically isolated as that other, and very different, terrorist movement—the IRA in Ireland.

THE PROVISIONAL IRA

The Provisional IRA, and the Protestant extremist movements which have been generated in reaction to it, are alone amongst terrorist organizations in the world, in that they are almost wholly devoid of intellectuals, even amongst the leaders. The few intellectuals who do support the Provisional IRA, such as the members of the International Marxist Group, seem to do so more for their own gratification than in response to any demand from the IRA for their help, and the members of the IRA, while accepting that help for what it is worth, find it embarrassing and do little to hide their contempt.[1]

The tragedy is that the IRA in its early days really did have a claim to the title of 'good guys', by virtue of being a nationalist movement fighting against foreign occupation. Its ill-timed Easter Rising in 1916 failed to attract popular support and ended in disaster, but it did create martyrs so that when Michael Collins revived the campaign in 1919 the majority of the Catholic Irish were sympathetic and this gave him the legitimacy he needed. He was then himself assassinated by the IRA in 1922 after he had triumphed in the war of independence and had negotiated the British withdrawal from Southern Ireland. The IRA killed him because he had accepted the compromise that

1. David O'Connell, a senior member of the Provisionals' Army Council, made this clear in a television interview shortly after Dr. Rose Dugdale had been tried and imprisoned in Dublin for offences which he and she admitted were in support of the Provisional IRA. Rank and file members of the Provisional IRA had taken part, but this appears to have been without the Provisional Army Council's approval, and rather to its embarrassment. B.B.C. *Midweek*, 3rd July 1974.

the six predominantly Protestant counties of the North should remain part of the United Kingdom. But despite the assassination of Collins, his party was re-elected and remained in power for the next ten years and is in power again now.

Thus from 1922 onwards the IRA was fighting *against* the government of the Republic of Ireland and against the majority of the Catholic Irish people who elected it; and it continued to do so whichever party was in power. Between 1956–62, when Collins' old opponent De Valera was Prime Minister, the IRA mounted its disastrous 'border campaign' in which it failed to attract support from the Catholics either North or South of the border. After this failure the old gun-toting IRA leadership was supplanted by a marxist leadership, whose main target was the overthrow of the system of parliamentary government in Dublin, and which hoped to unite rather than divide the Protestant and Catholic working classes in the North. This marxist movement still exists as the 'Official IRA' and is dedicated to political action rather than violence. For this reason it tried to stay aloof from the Protestant/Catholic fighting in the communal rioting in Belfast, in 1969. The old hardline IRA members felt that it had let down the Catholic community in its hour of need and formed their own Provisional IRA, rearming themselves during 1970 and launching an urban guerrilla campaign in 1971. As usual it was the civilians rather than the soldiers or guerrillas who suffered most. Of the 1,000 people killed up until May 1974, 310 were soldiers or policemen, 140 were IRA members and 550 (55 per cent) were ordinary members of the public—Irish men, women and children, Protestant and Catholic—killed mainly in bombings and in sectarian murders.

Even at the height of the violence in 1971–72 the IRA never enjoyed the support of more than 10 per cent of the Catholic population in the six counties of Northern Ireland and by the end of 1972 their apparently mindless bombing of the civilian population[2] had reduced this to around 3 per cent. By the middle of 1974 it was estimated by Cardinal Conway—the Catholic Primate of All Ireland—that this support had dwindled to a fraction of 1 per cent—with an equally tiny proportion of

2. See page 85.

Protestants supporting their own terrorist movements[3] (though a great many more supported the Ulster Workers' Council which said that it condemned violence). This had earlier been borne out in the Parliamentary elections, both in the South at the end of 1972, and in the North in 1973, where the votes for extremist candidates of any colour (and the number of abstentions or spoiled papers which the Provisional IRA recommended) were again of negligible proportions.[4] The IRA have never regained the legitimacy of popular support which they lost in 1922.

The Provisional IRA subscribe to no particular political theory. Their philosophy is based upon a combination of Marighela's and that of General Grivas in Cyprus. They hope, on the one hand, to provoke repression and 'make life unbearable' for the people in Northern Ireland itself; and, on the other hand, to sicken the British Government and the British people with the whole business so that they will cut their losses and get out. What would happen after that has not seriously been considered, because the political wing of the Provisional IRA is what has been described as little more than a propaganda department for the gunmen.[5]

Their political weakness was underlined by their failure to seize two golden opportunities to emerge as an open political party with the prestige to attract incomparably wider public support—in March 1972, when the British Government suspended the Protestant dominated Northern Ireland Parliament, and again in December 1973, when a Conference of the London and Dublin Governments (with representatives of the major Protestant and Catholic political parties from Belfast), signed the Sunningdale agreement proposing a unified Council of Ireland.[6]

3. B.B.C. Documentary 'Ulster—The Last Five Years', 29th July 1974.
4. See Richard Clutterbuck, *Protest and the Urban Guerrilla* (U.S. edition) (New York, Abelard-Schuman, 1974, p. 149).
5. Conor Cruise O'Brien, now a minister in the Dublin Coalition Government, reported in the *Observer* on 26th March 1972.
6. Austin Currie, a leading member of the Catholic Social Democratic and Labour Party, B.B.C., 'The Last Five Years', 29th July 1974.

They could have claimed credit for both, and would undoubtedly have been able to emerge with the freedom to do so, if they had called off the violence. Instead, they proved that they were not interested in political power, but only in the power of the gun. This attitude had also been the root of their earlier failures and had accounted for their lack of popular support since they declared war on their own Government in 1922.

THE INTELLECTUAL TERRORIST

Some of the rank and file of the Argentine ERP (and this could apply to other groups) may be found to come from deprived communities and from criminal gangs who are attracted by the prospects of ransom and can offer the services of their organizations and skills. The ERP leadership, however, insists upon the insertion of a party cell to control any such groups,[7] and this leadership is almost wholly intellectual. This is neither new nor surprising, nor does it differ from the business, commercial or bureaucratic world outside; nor is it confined to Latin America. Lenin, Mao, Castro, Guevara and Giap were all educated men. All of them, except Mao (a librarian), were university graduates and two were Doctors of Philosophy.

Most guerrilla leaders have had a relatively cultured and comfortable childhood. Michael Calvert, in a historical survey of 55 guerrilla leaders, found that over 90 per cent had more than average education and came from prosperous or middle-income families.[8] This continues to be the pattern.

Some guerrilla groups have been almost wholly composed of intellectuals, even the rank and file. This has included some quite large groups like the Tupamaros (3,000 strong in their day) and most of the small ones, like the German Baader Meinhof gang, the American Weathermen, the British Angry Brigade and the Japanese Red Army Fraction.

Why did these people, many with much to offer to the com-

7. See page 44.
8. Michael Calvert, 'The Characteristics of Guerrilla Leaders and their Rank and File', in *The Practitioner*, London, December 1973.

munity, turn to revolution and violence? What induced Lenin and Castro to throw away the prospect of successful careers as lawyers? Both of these, in the event, had still greater success and became heads of state, but the overwhelming majority of revolutionaries can look forward only to death, imprisonment, a life on the run and, usually, ultimate disillusion.

It is not, however, with this tiny proportion of men who are of the calibre to become successful revolutionaries and heads of state, that we should be primarily concerned. They have a political dedication which will transcend their own self-interest and the few who do not die will prevail. Nor, generally, do they resort to the kind of terrorism which this book is about, for they are shrewd enough to know that this will not pay.

The kidnapping, bombing and hijacking is generally done, not by successful revolutionaries, but by terrorists doomed to fail, whether they are poor and uneducated like the IRA, or from an affluent and educated background. The terrorist seldom brings progressive change—but only backlash. He creates nothing, but only kills and destroys. In extreme cases, like Okamoto, he will have no more regard for his own life than for those of others, and has no coherent or practical political aim.[9] He has more in common with the tragically ineffective Russian anarchists of the 1880s, than with Lenin or Trotsky or Mao or Giap. They all looked ahead to the kind of society they hoped to create, and to the practicalities of building it and running it after the revolutions, but the terrorist sees no further than his violent attack on the existing society. And usually—except in movements like the Palestinian guerrillas or the IRA—he has no burning sense of nationalism on which to focus his political beliefs.

There is nothing particularly abnormal about young people of independent spirit chafing against the dominance of the old, at home, at school and at work. But only a few extend this to the point of violence and terrorism, and these few are found from amongst the more affluent students at the universities and very seldom from amongst those who have made their way into university from a working-class family.

Part of the explanation may lie in a feeling of guilt about their

9. See page 113.

sheltered childhood and the privileges they enjoy. But there is also the fact that there seems to be no 'abyss' into which they will fall if they fail. Forty years ago a graduate leaving university could expect to earn several times more than if he were an unqualified manual worker. This is no longer so. In Britain today a graduate is lucky to earn more than £30 a week (£1,500 a year) in his first job. He could probably get £35 right away as a manual worker or £45 with overtime. If this fails, he has his father—or social security—to fall back on. He can therefore risk throwing away his 'advantages' and discarding the ethics and ambitions which his parents tried to inculcate in him.

This sense of security, which can be cloying, may also lead him to indulge in one of his most early, childhood desires—shocking his parents, and then shocking the society in which he finds himself.

Then follows the fulfilment of yet another impatient aspiration—calling a tune to which people will dance; and calling it *now*—not as a manager or as bureaucrat after a 30-year climb up the ladder of a structure, which he despises and rejects. At university he gets this kind of response from his fellow students. They *do* dance to his tune.

His rejection of the consumer society may be genuinely idealistic, and it is on the immature and idealistic personality that marxist indoctrination often has a disastrous effect. Having little first-hand knowledge of the proletariat he feels it his mission to liberate, he develops an unconscious contempt for them as 'unthinking sheep', who can be driven this way or that by the pressures of society's propaganda—and of his. He becomes convinced that he knows better than they themselves know, what they *ought* to want. He sees them as grey figures, swarming through factory gates—and not as men and women, whose average age is 45, who have children, and who have seen something of the world. Marxism is an ascetic doctrine devoid of warmth or sympathy and its effect on the immature and idealistic person is characteristic. He develops love for no one, feeling only hatred and contempt.

Out of every 100 students who succumb for a time to this indoctrination, probably only one or two are led to the point of becoming violent. These are often the ones with social or personality defects, who may feel rejected by their parents or by their contemporaries, or who are psychopathic. They are the ones around whom indoctrination builds a hard shell, imprisoning the human spirit, and within which—if not tackled in time—the vestiges of humanity will wither and die, leaving a Frankenstein monster, like Okamoto, dedicated only to a cold and pitiless violence.

A key moment in this horrifying destruction of a human being is when he becomes committed by, for example, killing a man or blowing up a building. After this, he cannot turn back. Aware of this, it is part of the technique of a terrorist leader to get his recruits so committed as early as possible.[10]

The recruit is then ready to be launched without reservation on to the 'cycle of Carlos Marighela', as described in Chapter 1. He aims to make it impossible for the government to maintain orderly life without harassment and repression, making life unbearable for the people, leading either to the chaos in which the terrorist can quickly seize power, or to an abrogation of power in favour of a weak government which will dance to the terrorists' tune, or to a backlash and further repression which will start the whole cycle off again.

10. An interesting side effect is that some criminal fraternities in the U.S.A. guard themselves against police penetration by requiring their initiates to kill a policeman before they are admitted.

Chapter Thirteen

Prevention and Cure

THE HUMAN BEING INSIDE THE SHELL

BEFORE drawing conclusions about the motivation and techniques of the terrorist and about how to contain his violence, it is worth devoting some attention to the problems of preventing him from becoming a terrorist, or of curing him of the disease. This can be no more than an introduction to a huge subject but in the long run these are the problems which must be solved if the world is to be rid of terrorism, and some understanding of them can help, in the short term, in the task of countering it.

In the case of the Palestinian and IRA terrorists there are deep nationalistic roots to the problem, requiring international political solutions. The Palestinian terrorists, however (though not the IRA), also have much in common psychologically with the other intellectual terrorists bred mainly in the universities.

The problem lies, as described in the last chapter, in the explosive effect which a marxist indoctrination can have on certain kinds of immature and idealistic personalities, especially on those suffering from personal or social inadequacies which deny them fulfilment in other ways. It is vitally important therefore to rescue the human spirit before it becomes imprisoned in the hard and vicious shell of the terrorist, and before the person has become irrevocably 'committed' by a crime of violence.

The heaviest responsibility must fall upon parents and teachers, and especially upon tutors at universities. Unfortunately a large proportion of teachers go direct to their school or university after graduating themselves, without the experience of anything more than a superficial contact with the main stream of working people outside. Many of them have selected teaching as a profession because they feel that they can exert most influence

134

if they can have access to the minds of the rising generation before these have become 'socialized' by the environment of the world outside. The problem may become self-perpetuating, because teachers become headmasters and lecturers become professors, still without ever having had their ideas tested by anything other than academic discussion with students and fellow teachers. Then, as senior staff, even further out of touch with the real world, they may recruit new staff in their own image.

There are various ways in which an antidote of realism might be infused into universities but none are without difficulties. Government grants could be conditional on a high percentage of staff having worked in the outside world for at least three years before being engaged. But this might, in practice, result in the universities getting only the rejects because those who had been successful in industry would never come back to teach. Another condition could be that a rising proportion of students—eventually half or more—should be 'mature students'—i.e., should themselves have spent three years outside before admission. But again many would by then have wives, children and good pay, and not be keen to go back and live on a grant unless the taxpayers were willing to make that grant comparable with average earnings in industry for someone of the same age.

It would be important, however, not to let the tail wag the dog. The proportion of students leaving university with the desire to disrupt society is very small and only a minute number of these are inclined towards violence. Over-reaction is in practice likely to increase these proportions. The answer lies rather in patiently fostering a climate of opinion amongst teachers and students than in applying strong institutional remedies. It is significant that the two nations most tolerant of dissidents have by far the longest records of survival for their constitutions— Britain (three centuries) and the U.S.A. (two). Few others can score more than 50 years.

Once again the world is indebted to Sir Geoffrey Jackson for pointing the way. Imprisoned and degraded for eight months by relays of Uruguayan student terrorists, he managed to reach through into the shells of at least some of them and to get a response from the human being still just alive inside. He did this by seeking and finding a common sense of humour, mixed with a very real compassion. He made them laugh, in spite of themselves, and even *at* themselves—though he never saw their faces behind the hoods they always wore. At least one young couple, their three weeks of guard duty over, reached their hands through the pig-wire to take his, and the girl told him: 'You will walk with us all our lives, Ambassador.'[1]

Tragically, most of the young Tupamaros in whom he revived a flicker of natural, human warmth have probably now been killed in the backlash which their movement eventually provoked, or are languishing, with growing embitterment and dwindling hope, in prison.

KEEPING OUT THE TERRORISTS AND THEIR WEAPONS

Until, or unless, he can be rescued or cured, however, the terrorist must be treated as a dangerous criminal. He must be prevented from getting the tools he needs to kill or destroy and, if he has those tools, he must be denied access to vulnerable places or vulnerable people.

In Chapter 5 we examined the means of keeping the terrorist out of buildings. In Chapter 7 we looked at ways of detecting the tools he uses for murder *in absentia*—his bombs, posted, dumped or detonated by remote control. In Chapter 11 we saw how successfully, in one country at least, he has been prevented from getting his tools through the airport lobby to board an aircraft.

There are, in addition, other and more general areas in which it may be possible to detect and apprehend him: by passport and immigration control; by introducing identity cards and applying stricter control of movement and lodging; and by police intelligence supported by public alertness and co-operation. All of these things involve some interference with personal freedom, but this may be a price, which a people under lethal attack from within, may be prepared to pay—as they have accepted being searched at the airport boarding gates.

A more serious problem is that all these measures offer opportunities for abuse. They may be introduced by unscrupulous

1. Jackson, *op. cit.* (p. 66).

governments who wish to tighten their control over their
population for other reasons and to give them an excuse they
create a fantasy of terrorism. They also place greater power in
the hands of governments and police forces and such power, once
gained, has a tendency both to corrupt and to grow. Society must
be as vigilant in guarding against such abuse and corruption,
as it is in guarding against the terrorism which created the need
(or the excuse) for tighter population control.

Passports are easy to forge. This can be made more difficult by
incorporating a magnetic card on which identification data is
recorded. Further data can be added—not necessarily with the
knowledge of the passport holder—recording, for example,
when and where he left and entered various countries. Passports
are also easily stolen,[2] but the magnetic card can guard against
this too. Immigration points can be equipped with an electromagnetic interrogator, exclusive to them and capable of decoding
the data and of making an immediate print-out. If the coded data
on the card is comprehensive, it is unlikely that the false bearer
of it will be able to survive cross-examination. Such a scheme,
however, would require international co-operation and would
cost money, manpower and time. If international terrorism
becomes a greater threat, governments and their peoples may be
willing to bear these costs.

Identity cards are alien to British and American society, but are
used in a great many others. They were also used, under British
administration, in countries faced with highly-organized terrorist
campaigns—e.g. in Malaya from 1948–57. They enable the police
to make at least an initial check, on the spot, as to whether a
person is who he claims to be, and can be coupled with some form
of *lodging registration*, whereby hotel and boarding-house keepers
or heads of households are required to register officially every
person who stays in their house even for a night. This is already a

2. There is a lucid and convincing account of both forgery and theft
   of passports by Frederick Forsyth in *The Day of the Jackal* (London, Corgi, 1971). Though written as fiction, this book is very close
   to fact. John Stonehouse, MP, used a similar method in 1974.

legal requirement in the Netherlands and in many other countries. Modern techniques would enable this data to be recorded much more quickly and efficiently than it could, for example, when it was in force under the Emergency Regulations in Malaya. If a terrorist threat, as grave as that in Malaya, were to hit Britain or the United States, a combination of identity cards and lodging registration would make it easier to detect and apprehend terrorists using 'safe houses' from which to operate in the cities.

Identity cards can, of course, be forged and the system can be disrupted if the underground organization is strong enough to carry out widespread theft and destruction of the cards under threat of violence. Also, of course, this scheme fails if there is a general public resistance to their use—though this is unlikely if there is genuine alarm about terrorism. A deterrent to destruction is to impose a regulation that retailers are legally required to sell the necessities of life, such as food or fuel, only on production of the card. The holders will then resist pressure to destroy them because of the inconvenience they would suffer. Forgery can also be guarded against by the use of magnetically coded data as described for passports.

There are many other kinds of data which can be recorded. This amounts to an extension of the *police records* system for criminals. Anyone convicted of a crime is likely to have certain of his particulars held in police files in case he is wanted for questioning about a future crime. These are likely to include his photograph, his fingerprints, his date of birth, where he has lived, and his past associates (who may be called in to identify him or to whom he might turn if he is on the run). These are, at present, hedged with various safeguards. If, for example, the fingerprints of a suspect are taken for comparison with fingerprints on the scene of a crime, and the suspect is not convicted, the records of his prints are legally required to be destroyed. In a real state of terrorist siege, there might be a demand to record all such particulars for anyone or even for everyone, with public support as strong as the support for searching of airline passengers.

This would, however, be the thin end of a very unpleasant wedge, and a large step towards what is generally known as a 'police state'. Other *emergency regulations* might include tight restrictions on the possession of arms (always in force in Britain but not in the U.S.A.) and severe penalties for unauthorized possession; increased powers of search, arrest and detention and if necessary, modification of trial procedures to protect witnesses and juries from intimidation or attack; the creation of new offences under the law: against, for example, intimidation, espionage or the harbouring of wanted men; against membership of proscribed organizations or possession or distribution of literature prepared by, or supporting, such organizations. There could even be an erosion of the principle of confidentiality of information, possessed professionally by doctors, bankers and priests.

CONVICTION AND SENTENCE

The most effective of deterrents against terrorism is, of course, a high rate of detection, conviction and punishment. This depends on the presentation of evidence, which in turn, depends upon the strength and quality of the police force, and the public confidence and support which it enjoys.

Detection and conviction were the aims of the Prevention of Terrorism (Temporary Provisions) Act passed by Parliament in Britain after the pub bombings in Birmingham in November 1974. Membership of the IRA and support for it (by, for example, demanding or subscribing money to it or organizing or addressing meetings or wearing or carrying things signifying support of it) became criminal offences. The police were empowered, subject to approval in each case by the Home Secretary, to hold suspects for questioning for up to seven days instead of a maximum of 48 hours. There were also increased powers of search at sea and air ports and of deportation.

Demands for other measures, such as the issue of identity cards, were resisted. And despite a public clamour for capital punishment for terrorists this too was rejected by a large majority in Parliament. There were strong grounds for rejection, since capital punishment confers not only martyrdom but glamour, and glamour is the best of all recruiters amongst the minute field from which terrorists—and their supporters—are drawn. Indiscriminate terrorism, such as in Birmingham, arouses the fury of the overwhelming majority of the public but if, in response to this fury, penalties are imposed which to a minority seem savage, more of that minority will feel some sympathy for the terrorist. In particular, if a young terrorist on the run faces execution, people may be more reluctant to give him away to the police. Juries, too, will be less ready to convict him. So the death penalty is likely to result in fewer rather than more convictions.

When such fury is aroused, the art of government lies in avoiding over reaction whilst being firm enough to prevent an exasperated public from taking the law into their own hands. Arrests and convictions are the best appeasers of public anger against terrorists. Despite the difficulties of finding needles in haystacks, the number of arrests and convictions after the M62, Guildford, Woolwich and Birmingham bombings in 1974 was very high. Intelligence was undoubtedly good and members of the public were clearly doing their utmost to help the police.

HELPING THE POLICE

More drastic measures—such as trial without jury for scheduled offences, and provision for detention without trial, where witnesses are openly intimidated—have had to be introduced in Northern Ireland, but not, thankfully, in Britain or the U.S.A. To keep this so, the primary defence is for the public to co-operate with the police, and especially with the police intelligence organization—Special Branch. Like the sharp-eyed London Transport railwayman who spotted the shopping bag bomb on Baker Street Station, the public can be the eyes and ears of Special Branch, drawing attention to suspicious behaviour, suspicious packages, suspicious arrivals and departures, suspicious cars, and suspicious houses, garages, workshops or warehouses which they think might be in use as 'safe houses' from which terrorists operate or plan to operate. Such reports will result in no more than investigation. If the investigation proves negative, nothing is lost but police manhours. If it is positive, it may provide the clue that will save a life.

Chapter Fourteen

Conclusions

THE GROWING THREAT

TERRORISM is almost sure to increase. It will increase primarily because, in the short term, it seems to pay; political blackmail gets results: convicted terrorists are released, huge ransoms are paid, and publicity, on a scale unimaginable before the television age, is acquired free.

It will increase, secondly, because industrial society becomes more vulnerable every day. Fifty years ago, a power stoppage would have been little more than a nuisance. Today it can cause immediate unemployment and the loss of millions of pounds worth of the community's production and reserves and of the goods which it exports to earn its living. It can deprive the community of food, warmth, water and drainage and quickly reduce it to chaos and disease. In cold weather people will die.

Public transport is just as vulnerable. Right-wing terrorists in Italy killed 12 people by blowing up a train in August 1974. Left-wing terrorists blew up 55 people in a Swiss Airlines jet aircraft in 1970. The IRA tried, but luckily failed, to blow up an aircraft in July 1974 in which 92 people would have died. The blowing up of a Jumbo could kill 400.

Terrorism will also increase because terrorists can travel more and more easily. As their funds are built up, by ransoms and robberies and (in the case of the Palestinians) by contributions from some of the rich Arab oil states, air fares will worry them no more than bus fares worried an anarchist in the 1880s. Okamoto and his comrades travelled two-thirds of the way round the world—first-class—to kill their 24 fellow-passengers at Lod Airport in May 1972.

Terrorist ideas travel even more easily than the terrorists

141

themselves. Their underlying politics—not initially violent, but carrying the seeds of violence—are disseminated in student meetings and cells in universities all over the world. Ample funds again, provide for the printing and circulation of their writings on a massive scale; for the financing of radio stations and for the provision of transistor radios with which to receive their broadcasts; also for the making and distribution of lavishly produced films, in colour, for world-wide screening on television and in cinemas. Also, violence is news, so 'armed propaganda'—the staging of incidents which will attract the attention of the media—gives free and vivid publicity to the terrorists, and brings their actions and ideas to the attention of an audience so vast that, even if the overwhelming majority reject them, the tiny proportion in whom they may strike a chord of sympathy amounts to a lot of people all over the world.

As well as receiving support from foreign governments, terrorist groups, as they get both richer and better informed, co-operate increasingly with each other. An IRA or Palestinian terrorist wanting to mount an operation to blow up the Tower of London or to shoot down aircraft taking off from London Airport can, through a normal screen of cut-off men, quickly make contact with groups in Britain which will provide him (if he needs them) with guns, ammunition, explosives, material for fuse mechanisms, stolen cars, false number plates, guides, telephone facilities, logistical support and—above all—a 'safe house' from which to mount his operation.

PERSONAL PROTECTION

The terrorist often kills indiscriminately, but his terrorism is more effective when it is aimed at selected individuals.

The individual is subject to attack by kidnapping, shooting, bombing or hijacking. If he is a statesman or the head of a very large firm, it may be possible for him to be provided with enough protection to deter attack. Even in a country where the fabric of law and order is intact and where it is hazardous for terrorists to deploy more than half a dozen units of half a dozen men each, on a single operation, nothing less than a guard of about forty, distributed in widely-separated cars and backed by a well-organized police force on immediate call by radio, can provide adequate protection from kidnapping on the road.

Ordinary mortals do not have forty men to protect them. Ambassadors and senior executives might get three or four. Most people—and everyone down to the junior clerk may be vulnerable as a potential hostage—can expect none. They must rely on the general framework of public security. But there is a lot that they can do to take care of themselves.

If they are to live a normal open life with their families, as part of the community and committed to travelling the open road to work, they can do much to help themselves, by being mentally 'tuned in' to the threat and by understanding how a kidnapping is mounted. Provided that they keep a low profile and avoid routine, varying their journeys, and their times and their habits, a kidnap operation will need more reconnaissance and planning than most people think. The indicators of such reconnaissance and planning can be spotted by someone who knows what to look for.

If the risk becomes too great to accept, potential victims may have to be collectively housed in defended compounds and have to move in protected convoys. Though this involves paying a price in isolation from the community, and means a sacrifice of quality of life, it has been done often enough when the situation required it, and it works.

The man in a responsible position in a society under terrorist attack, the front-line soldier of today, can do much to reduce his own attractiveness as a target and—as every soldier knows—the enemy will always be ready to look for another mug. If he is captured, there is no substitute for courage and endurance. Men have shown that drugging, interrogation by the most devilish of modern psychological techniques, and even torture, can be endured. There are ways in which the victim can maintain his judgement, his integrity, his spirit, his dignity, despite his degradation and—above all—his mental and physical health. Everyone has a breaking point but some have proved how deep the reserves of the human spirit can be. In so doing, they have learned a lot about terrorists and about how they operate, and have made what they have learned available for the world to use.

PROTECTION OF BUILDINGS

No hardware, however expensive, can rival the eyes, ears, hands and brains of a man. Hardware can, however, enable each man to cover more ground and, in the long run, the hardware probably saves more than it costs. Hardware is also less liable to fall asleep and can be fitted with an alarm which attracts attention if it does.

Fixed barriers—locks, fences, walls and lights—provide the framework. Electrical, electronic, infra-red, photo-electric, magnetic and mechanical devices can detect movement, body-heat, weight, impact, tampering and vibration, and can signal their detection to one man at a central point who can call out others. Much is available to those who ask.

BOMBS

The bomb is the meanest of weapons. It kills indiscriminately and without risk to the terrorist—once he has assembled and placed it. There is no certain defence, but the potential victim can again do much to protect himself by understanding how the various types of bombs and of fuses are set up and used. He need only know enough about neutralizing them to know when it is best to call in an expert to do this.

He can, however, contribute a great deal more to his own defence, and to the defence of others, by an alert understanding of the ways of the bomber, and about what kind of things are suspicious about a package, or a car, or the behaviour of a man.

Indiscriminate bombing is also self-defeating in the end. It discredits the cause of its perpetrators and arouses more public hostility, and hence public alertness, than any other form of attack, though there is a danger of public apathy, if it is allowed to become too familiar.

BLACKMAIL AND RANSOM

In the long run it never pays to give way to blackmail. In the short run this principle is easier to enunciate than to practise. It is unlikely that the British public would have supported Mr Heath as Prime Minister in September 1970, if he had handed Leila Khaled over in custody to the Israelis at the price of a large party of unaccompanied British children being blown up in the desert at Dawson's Field.

Nevertheless, where firmness has been used, it has paid. The British Government stood firm over its kidnapped diplomats, Jasper Cross and Geoffrey Jackson, in 1970–71 and this deterred other diplomatic kidnappings. The American Government stood firm against a far bigger threat and American diplomats paid a bigger price. Of 27 kidnapped diplomats, 10 were murdered, but most American foreign service-men agree that, but for this firm stand, many more would have been kidnapped, and many more killed.

Largely as a result of this government firmness, American business executives overseas seem largely to have taken over from American diplomats in the front line against terrorism. It is hard to defend the readiness of some commercial firms to pay ransoms, for this has certainly increased the incentive for kidnapping, as well as providing vast funds for future operations. Nevertheless, this is a moving battle and—as was shown in Brazil in 1971—it can be won against all the odds, though at a price for the community which many would not wish to pay.

HIJACKING

In 1969–70 there seemed to be no defence against hijacking, but the cost of failing to cure it was so high and the hurt to the public so grievous, that the country hardest hit—the United States— decided that it must be tackled. The task of searching every one of 150 million passengers per year, each with hand- and hold-baggage, to prevent a single pistol or grenade slipping through

K

the net, seemed impossible, but it was attempted and—almost incredulously—America saw hijacking dwindle to negligible proportions in 1973 and 1974.

Whether hijacking revives or not, the American experience has proved that, with determination, the most intractable of terrorist techniques can be defeated, and this is deeply encouraging.

THE TERRORIST DISEASE

Some terrorists, such as the Palestinians and the IRA, are driven by a burning nationalism. Thus far they have been blind to the fact that terrorism has retarded their cause. When they do realize this (and some may be realizing it already) they can be expected to modify their tactics, as their cause, whether justified or not, is a real one.

Most other terrorist groups have no such specific political cause. The ERP have shown this in Argentina, where they have attacked the Peronist Government for whose return they campaigned as violently as they attacked its predecessors. Some of the most vicious (like the Italian neo-fascists) are right-wing, but the majority subscribe to various forms of marxism or anarchism. Their creed is negative—to destroy society as it is, but without having any clear idea of what they want to substitute in its place. Violence and disruption, in themselves, provide their main satisfaction. Unlike the nationalist movements, therefore, they are unlikely to cure themselves or to be cured by a discovery that logic shows their activities to be counter-productive.

This kind of terrorist is, in the end, likely to be more vicious, and is less easy to forgive. He has almost always, in practice, had the benefit of an education, denied to most of those on whose behalf he claims he is killing; he comes from a background more comfortable than theirs, and has voluntarily discarded a life more rewarding than theirs; and he is almost universally rejected by them.

Generally his indoctrination has imprisoned his humanity in an artificial, terrorist identity and may eventually kill it altogether. The number on whom the indoctrination has this effect is very, very small, but it is this small number who can do most harm, so it is vitally important to prevent this happening. This is a task which must be persevered with by parents, schools, universities, employers and, ultimately, by the very people who are the victims of their terrorism.

Some intellectual terrorist groups do also recruit rank and file from amongst the poor and deprived. Sometimes the aim is 'image-building'; to create evidence that they do represent the people. White terrorist groups in the U.S.A., for example, try to recruit blacks for this purpose. More often the 'proletarian' recruits are bitter and desperate drop-outs who can find nowhere else to turn. And now, increasingly, the pickings from ransoms and bank-robberies are attracting the criminal world.

The Government and the Media

The overwhelming proportion of the public detest terrorism and want themselves and their families to be protected against it. It is important for governments to remember this, and to keep it always before the public eye. Terrorists are *taught* to use the media; governments are less good at it. The media want news and, while the terrorists can provide them with this by their 'armed propaganda', the government and its agencies can give the media more positive help in getting at the news. They can, for example, notify reporters and cameramen when and where action is likely to occur or has occurred and help them to get themselves and their equipment to positions of advantage. If the government does this, the news will usually take care of itself and will have a favourable slant—because editors and producers will wish to strike a chord with their readers and viewers who, they know, deplore terrorism and sympathize with its victims, and with the soldiers or policemen who fight it.

The television camera is like a weapon lying in the street. Either side can pick it up and use it. If governments use it in this way—encouraging their officials, policemen and soldiers to help the media-men, and to answer their question—it is far more effective than any kind of censorship or government control.

The Law, the Police and the Public

The law in a free society was evolved in the first place to protect the community from its anti-social members and, more gradually thereafter, to defend the freedom of the individual and to protect him from persecution, either by stronger organizations within society or by the state itself. One of the most significant, and one of the oldest, laws in Anglo-Saxon society is that of habeas corpus. Without it, a person, innocent or guilty, could vanish without trace, and this can still happen in most countries of the world.

In the face of a calculated and violent attack, with the aim of destroying society as it stands, the first category of laws—those protecting the community—may have to be strengthened and the second category—those protecting the freedom of the individual —may have to be modified by emergency legislation. It is important that such legislation should be temporary, publicly enacted, and subject to review.

The need for such legislation can best be avoided by encouraging and facilitating the maximum possible co-operation between the police and the public, and by strictly guarding against corruption of the police. To foster corruption is always a prime terrorist aim, because if the police corruptly connive at their activities they have greater scope, while if the police are corrupt in other ways they can be discredited. Either suits the terrorist very well. The attraction of high-quality recruits to the police force and the payment of salaries, generous enough to remove the temptation of corruption, are fundamentally important.

The public rely on the police for protection, and the police rely on the public for information. The marriage between an uncorrupt police force and an alert and co-operative public is the healthiest guard against terrorism.

The Danger of Over-Reaction

Ultimately a terrorist threat—the threat of a weak minority using stealth and violence to dominate a strong majority—can always be defeated by *force majeur*, but this must be applied with restraint. It has been done successfully in some countries in Latin America and elsewhere, but at a heavy cost in quality of life and in the creation of a brittle structure and a rumbling resentment which may presage a violent explosion at some time in the future. A civilization which can accommodate dissent has a better prospect of prolonged survival.

One of the most urgent reasons for keeping down terrorism is to ensure that we are not faced with the introduction of Draconian measures as the only alternative to death, destruction and chaos— the kind of 'repression' which Carlos Marighela exhorts his disciples to provoke.

Over-reaction would not only poison our way of life, it would also play into the terrorists' hands, by building more public sympathy for them, and by increasing what is now only a tiny trickle of recruits to their ranks.

On the other hand, if a government fails to protect its citizens, those citizens may take the law into their own hands by forming, first, vigilante groups and then, as law and order breaks down, their own private armies. This was the road to Nazism.

The likeliest result of uncontrolled terrorism is not that it will bring unwanted or revolutionary change, but that it will bring a backlash—either a government backlash or a backlash by an exasperated public, responding to a call by right-wing demagogues to rally for their own defence.

In any case, ultimately, the result would be the same. If right-wing terrorists (like the Italian neo-fascists or the Provisional IRA) or left-wing terrorists (like the PFLP or the ERP) were to gain control, personal freedom under the law would vanish, probably for ever. If, in reaction to either of these extremes, a backlash were to lead to the emergence of a military or police dictatorship, the individual would be subject to state terror instead of clandestine terror. By whichever route it arrived, society would take on the ugly shape so vividly foretold in George Orwell's *Animal Farm* and *1984*, and well described in Alexander Solzhenitzyn's *Gulag Archipelago*.

Men have shown over the centuries that they can live with terrorism and can ultimately defeat it without sacrificing their freedom. Some have died in trying to do so. In the face of the violence of a small number of people, who wish to cast out a free, but mutually-responsible society in favour of either the jungle of the anarchist or the ant-hill of the marxist state, there is a temptation to seek refuge in the alternative of the fascist state. The middle course of continuing to improve the concept of a tolerant, co-operative and civilized community, which has taken thousands of years to develop, is more difficult to follow, but more worthwhile. This is what the greatest number of people want, and it is the overwhelming rejection of the terrorist by the greatest number which must be harnessed to defend it.

Select Bibliography

THERE is a vast amount of literature about terrorism and counter-terrorism and there are also comprehensive bibliographies available. I have made a selection of writings which I hope will be the most useful in giving the feel of this type of conflict. I have included some allegorical or fictional writing (e.g. Orwell and Forsyth) as this adds a dimension which fact or analysis cannot always provide, just as a painting sometimes tells the truth better than a photograph.

ARENDT, Hannah, *On Violence* (London, Penguin, 1970)

BOULTON, David, *The UVF 1966–73* (Dublin, Torc Books, 1973)

BURNS, Alan, *The Angry Brigade* (London, Quartet, 1973)
    A vivid picture of the lives of six people who lived in a commune and turned to violence. Written as fiction, it is based on factual tape-recordings by the author, who is a lawyer.

CALVERT, Michael, 'The Characteristics of Guerrilla Leaders and their Rank and File' in *The Practitioner* (London, December 1973)

CLUTTERBUCK, Richard, *Protest and the Urban Guerrilla* (London, Cassell, 1973; and New York, Abelard-Schuman, 1974)

CLYNE, Peter, *An Anatomy of Skyjacking* (London, Abelard-Schuman, 1973)

CONGRESSIONAL COMMITTEE STAFF STUDY, *Political Kidnappings 1968–73* (Washington, 1973)

CROZIER, Brian (ed.), *Annual of Power and Conflict* (London, Inst. for Study of Conflict, 1974)

CROZIER, Brian, *A Theory of Conflict* (London, Hamish Hamilton, 1974)

DEBRAY, Régis, *Revolution in the Revolution?* (London, Penguin, 1968)

DILLON, M. and LEHANE, D., *Political Murder in Northern Ireland* (London, Penguin, 1973)

FANON, Frantz, *The Wretched of the Earth* (London, Penguin, 1967)

FORSYTH, Frederick, *The Day of the Jackal* (London, Corgi, 1971)
    A fictional account of an assassination attempt on de Gaulle, with some authentic details about how international terrorists work and of how policemen try to catch them.

GILIO, Maria Esther, *The Tupamaros* (London, Secker & Warburg, 1972)

JACKSON, Geoffrey, *People's Prison* (London, Faber and Faber, 1972), also published as *Surviving the Long Night* (New York, Vanguard, 1974)

JANKE, Peter, 'Terrorism in Argentina' in the *RUSI Journal* (London, September 1974)

JOHNSON, K., *Guatemala: From Terrorism to Terror* (London: Inst. for Study of Conflict, 1972)

JOHNSON, K., *Peronism: The Final Gamble* (London: Inst. for Study of Conflict, 1974)

KITSON, Frank, *Low Intensity Operations* (London, Faber and Faber, 1971)

MARIGHELA, Carlos, *For the Liberation of Brazil* (London, Penguin, 1971)

McKNIGHT, Gerald, *The Mind of the Terrorist* (London, Michael Joseph, 1974)

MOSS, Robert, *Urban Guerrillas* (London, Temple Smith, 1972)

ORWELL, George, *Animal Farm* and *1984* (Penguin editions)
    The most vivid and convincing picture available, in allegorical and fictional form, of the horrors of life under dictatorship, and of how liberation leads to even greater repression if the liberators are not themselves restrained by checks and balances.

PHILLIPS, David, *Skyjack* (London, Harrap, 1973)

PRIESTLAND, Gerald, *The Future of Violence* (London, Hamish Hamilton, 1974)

SOLZHENITZYN, A., *The Gulag Archipelago* (London, Collins/Fontana, 1974)

SOREL, Georges, *Reflections on Violence* (published 1906) (London, Collier, 1969)

WILKINSON, Paul, *Political Terrorism* (London, Macmillan, 1974)

Index